Workers' Co-operatives: A Handbook

WORKERS' CO-OPERATIVES:
A HANDBOOK

Peter Cockerton
Tim Gilmour-White
John Pearce
Anna Whyatt

ABERDEEN PEOPLE'S PRESS IN ASSOCIATION WITH
THE AUTHORS

Aberdeen People's Press Ltd., 163 King Street, Aberdeen, Scotland

Published by Aberdeen People's Press
in conjunction with the authors

Copyright © the authors 1980

Typeset and printed by Aberdeen People's Press Ltd. (T.U.)

ISBN 0 906074 06 1 paper
ISBN 0 906074 07 X cloth

Distributed by Scottish and Northern Books Distribution Co-operative Ltd., 45/47 Niddry Street, Edinburgh EH1 1LG. Tel. 031 557-0133 and Birchcliffe Centre, Hebden Bridge, West Yorkshire HX7 8DG. And by Southern Distribution, 27 Clerkenwell Close, London EC1 OAT. Tel. 01-251-4976.

Copies available from Aberdeen People's Press Ltd., at cover price plus 30p post.

CONTENTS

FOREWORD

PART I: WORKERS' CO-OPERATIVES IN BRITAIN   9

PART II: THE MECHANICS OF WORKERS' CO-OPERATIVES   17

   1. What are the principles of a workers' co-operative?   17

   2. Who can start a workers' co-operative?   19

   3. What might a workers' co-operative do?   20

   4. What commitment is required?   23

   5. What is involved in membership?   26

   6. Why is a legal structure desirable and what form of legal structure is most appropriate?   28

   7. How is a workers' co-operative organised?   36

   8. What finance does a workers' co-operative need?   43

   9. How do co-operative principles affect the financial structure of a workers' co-operative?   46

   10. What happens to the profits?   51

   11. How can associations of workers' co-operatives be formed?   54

   12. Epilogue   60

PART III: THE FUTURE FOR WORKER
CO-OPERATION IN BRITAIN   61

CASE STUDIES
1. A plant hire and building co-operative   69
2. Recycles   71
3. Calverts North Star Press   72
4. Triangle Wholefoods Collective (Suma)   74
5. The Mondragon organisation   76

APPENDICES
Appendix A: List of resources and addresses   79

Appendix B: Procedure for Registration as a
Co-operative under the Industrial and
Provident Societies Acts using the ICOM
Model Rules, with copy of the rules   85

Appendix C: Copy of Form F 617 - Industrial
and Provident Societies Act 1965 -
Registration of Societies   96

Appendix D: Notes on the Industrial Common
Ownership (ICO) Act, with copy of the Act   100

Appendix E: Examples of budgets, with notes   109

Appendix F: Industrial Common Ownership
Finance Ltd. Information for Loan Applicants,
Prospectus Requirements, Copy of Loan
Application Form and Department of
Industry guidelines for assessing projects   115

Appendix G: Selected bibliography about co-
operation and co-operatives   122

FOREWORD

This handbook first appeared in May 1977 as a Scottish Handbook published by the Scottish Council of Social Service in association with the Scottish Co-operatives Development Committee. The Foreword to that first edition said:

'A surge of interest in workers' co-operatives is currently evident throughout Britain. This reflects a search for new forms of industrial organisation which are more rewarding for those who work in them than private enterprise or nationalised industries. A workers' co-operative is controlled on a one person, one vote basis by the people working in it; the workers are collectively responsible for the direction of their enterprise'.

That interest in co-operation has continued, and there are now more than 300 known workers' co-operatives trading in Britain. The Scottish Handbook has gained a reputation as the most comprehensive available that was both practical and easy to read. As stocks of the original publication ran down it was decided to produce a U.K. edition, revised according to recent legislative and other changes and in the light of usage in the field by co-operators and co-operative advisers.

This handbook comprises three parts with seven appendices. Part I outlines the history of industrial co-operation in Britain and the contribution which workers' co-operatives might make to the solution of our present social and economic ills. Part II examines in detail the problems of establishing and running workers' co-operatives, covering such aspects as legal structure, internal organisation, management and finance. Part III considers the future role and importance of worker co-operation in the British economy as we enter the 1980s. The appendices include a comprehensive list of resource agencies and addresses, examples of simple budgets, a bibliography and further information about co-operative registration, the ICOM Model Rules, the ICO Act and ICOF loans.

Most of the material for the first edition was researched and written by Tim Gilmour-White. This revised and extended edition has been prepared by Peter Cockerton, John Pearce and Anna Whyatt working with Tim Gilmour-White. The authors would like to thank the Scottish Council of Social Service for permitting them to undertake the revision and re-publication of the Handbook and also Chaz Ball for his advice and assistance on the practical matters of production and distribution.

Peter Cockerton, Tim Gilmour-White
John Pearce, Anna Whyatt

October 1979

I. WORKERS' CO-OPERATIVES IN BRITAIN

The history of co-operation in Britain starts at the end of the 18th Century, when groups of working men in various parts of the country set up co-operative corn mills to break the monopoly of the millers. Early in the following century Robert Owen showed at New Lanark that it was possible to run a large cotton mill at a profit without the total exploitation and degradation of the workforce which was almost universal at that time. His success and tireless propaganda inspired the developing working class movement of the eighteen-twenties and thirties which hoped to organise production in 'co-operative home colonies', and it was this movement which led to the founding of the Rochdale Equitable Pioneers' Society in 1844.

The Pioneers' example, and pressure from the growing trade union movement, encouraged the setting up of many workers' co-operatives during the second half of the 19th Century, but by 1900 only about 100 remained, and to-day there are about 8 affiliated to the Co-operative Productive Federation, which is the trade association for producer co-operatives within the traditional Co-op Movement.

In seeking an answer as to why workers' co-operatives have fared so badly, it is useful to go back to the original intentions of the Rochdale Pioneers, the acknowledged founders of the British Co-op Movement and the inspiration for many such movements in other countries.

The Pioneers are generally remembered for their famous store in Toad Lane, Rochdale, i.e. for their retail activities, but to them the store was only a small part of their overall scheme. Their 1844 objectives read as follows:

1. The establishment of a store for the sale of provisions, clothing, etc.
2. The building, purchasing or erecting a number of houses in which those members, desiring to assist each other in improving their domestic and social conditions, may reside.
3. To commence the manufacture of such articles as the Society may determine upon, for the employment of such members as may be without employment, or who may be suffering in consequence of repeated reductions in their wages.
4. As a further benefit and security to the members of this Society, the Society shall purchase or rent an estate or estates of land, which shall be cultivated by the members who may be out of employment, or whose labour may be badly remunerated.
5. That, as soon as practicable, this society shall proceed to arrange the powers of production, distribution, education, and Government, or, in other words, to establish a self-supporting home colony of limited interests, or assist other societies in establishing such colonies.

By 1860 they owned at least two spinning mills and wrote that the purpose of their Society was 'that its members may have the profits arising from the employment of their own capital and labour in the manufacturing of cotton and woollen fabrics and so improve their social and domestic condition.' They set up social institutions, particularly for the relief of distress caused by illness, death and alcoholism, and their ideal, inherited from Owen, was a community which would give men equal rights as producers, consumers and citizens. This altruistic scheme, had it followed the course envisaged by the Society's founders, would have led to a British Co-operative Movement very different from the one we see to-day.

In order to raise capital the Society sold shares to non-co-operators among the general public, and by 1862 the workers' right to profit sharing had been abolished by a vote of the new shareholders, concerned much more about the size of their dividend than about the principles of co-operation.

By the mid-1950's the Co-op Movement, comprising the Co-operative Wholesale Society and more than 400 retail societies, was operating a system which has been called, perhaps unfairly, consumers' capitalism.

Whatever it may be called, and whatever view may be taken of its merits, it bears little relation to the intentions of the Movement's founders in Rochdale, which somehow came to be ignored, or perhaps forgotten, as the movement developed.

In the last decade, however, there has been a resurgence of interest in Britain in the idea of greater workers' control of industry. This has its roots in the wave of closures, amalgamations and redundancies associated with the 'rationalisation' of British industry in the 1960's and in the growing demands by the public for an increased say in industrial affairs. Rank and file trade unionists have become progressively less willing to negotiate redundancy agreements as they realise that alternative employment is not available. They have been searching for more effective means of fighting redundancy than the traditional strike which, if anything, helps rather than hinders factory closures, and that such means should be found is equally in the interest of employers. The public, less closely involved than the unions and employers, are nevertheless alarmed by inflation and massive unemployment, and disillusioned with what they see as divisive and time-wasting confrontation and apparently ineffectual tinkering with the economy by successive governments; they feel instinctively that 'there must be some other way'. The idea of workers' co-operatives springs naturally at the present time, as it has in the past, from such pressures and desires for industrial change, and this idea is just as relevant to the small enterprise starting from scratch as it is to the great 'redundancy battles' publicised by the media.

One person, one vote has been accepted for some generations as the proper way of organising our political system. The nation's jobs, however, remain by and large outwith similar democratic control, yet it is the weekly income which is the fundamental need of any family. As major enterprises which account for much of our employment become even larger and more international, decisions taken in the board-rooms of Washington, Brussels and Zurich, let alone London, can affect the future prospects and well-being of small towns and districts throughout Britain and indeed all over the western world.

In 1971 the collapse of Rolls Royce, hitherto synonymous with stability and security, highlighted the dependence of thousands of workers, their families and their communities on the activities of one company over which they had no control. The government of the day recognised that, whatever the cause, be it the failings of management or the hazards of the market, industrial communities should not be devastated by such a collapse. Rolls Royce was nationalised and thus saved.

Nationalisation, however, does not give employees increased control or influence over an enterprise. The management of nationalised industries has usually been in the style of the more autocratic types of private enterprise, and this form of collective ownership has given workers no increased control over organisation, policy or objectives.

Since the 1960's Britain has witnessed a growing demand by ordinary people for greater involvement in and control over those things which concern and affect their daily lives. Action groups have challenged local councils about social and community matters, demanding consultation, improved services and greater participation in decision making. Big has not been seen as necessarily better; rather it has been seen as remote and bureaucratic. People have demanded devolution of power from the centre. Throughout the United Kingdom there are demands for a 'say'.

In industry these demands have been slower to develop. The sit-in at Upper Clyde in 1971 demonstrated a new way of protesting against plans for closure and redundancy. At the same time the 'Fakenham Ladies' in Norfolk turned the protest of a work-in into the creation of their own business; a workers' co-operative. Since then other groups have responded to closure with the thought that 'if they can't do it, perhaps we can'.

The corollary of wanting a greater say is to do something yourself. The workers' co-operative is the industrial form of self-help and in the last three years more than 300 new workers' co-operatives have started trading in Britain.

These new co-operatives are operating in both the service and manufacturing industries, from wholefood shops to precision engineering, from restaurants to printing, from magazine distribution to food processing, from building to bicycle repair and hire. On the whole they are small enterprises but together they represent a growing number of jobs and are slowly establishing a new credibility for the ideals of co-operation. Sadly, it is not the success of the small co-operatives but the failures and problems of the big experiments to create co-operation out of failed capitalism which have attracted most attention in the media. It was a brave attempt in 1974/75 for Government to support the co-operative developments at Meriden, Kirkby and the Scottish Daily News but the experience of those three very unique situations should not mask the successful effort and struggle of the many other groups around the country. To start an enterprise, any enterprise, from a run-down or failed situation is anywhere fraught with particular and great difficulties.

The co-operative is a working community. In it, the profit motive is allied to a collective concern; concern on the one hand that the working members are adequately cared for and on the other that the co-operative is playing a constructive part in the wider community.

Conventional industry, as it becomes more capital intensive, replaces people with machines and provides jobs which are increasingly dull and repetitive. By contrast the co-operative will resist the need for redundancies, if necessary by agreeing a collective wage reduction at times of crisis. It will seek to make both work and working environment interesting and pleasant. Genuine worker control can give even the humblest worker a sense of involvement and belonging.

As part of wider society the co-operative is more likely to be sensitive to the needs of the community in which its members live. Profits which go to workers and to creating a viable work-providing enterprise rather than to outside shareholders are contributing towards the stability and security of the local community, and many co-operatives recognise a commitment to social objectives which benefit wider society.

The co-operative sector can be viewed as the 'third arm' in industry alongside private and state ownership, in much the same way as the Housing Association movement sees itself in the field of housing; fulfilling a useful and important practical role at the same time as influencing attitudes and practices generally. Self-managed co-operatives not only provide employment, but in doing so demonstrate that groups of working people can run industrial enterprises both democratically and successfully.

It will be a pity if the new initiatives towards workers' self-management suffer the same fate as did those of the Rochdale Pioneers, but there are signs that they need not do so, because there are now agencies sympathetic to their ideals which did not exist in the 19th Century.

The Industrial Common Ownership Act of 1976 has laid down legal definitions of common-ownership and co-operative enterprises which should be a safeguard against the dilution of ideals which bedevilled the Pioneers. The same Act provides a modest amount of grant aid for five years for Advisory Agencies which has for the most part been allocated between the Industrial Common Ownership Movement and the Scottish Co-operatives Development Committee. It also provides over the same periol a £1/4m loan fund which is administered through Industrial Common Ownership Finance Limited.

In the past two years there has been a striking growth of local bodies committed to giving help and support to co-operatives in their areas. In some cases these local Co-operative Development Groups are consortiums of a range of local interests - community groups, trade unionists, the 'traditional' co-operative movement, local workers' co-operatives, the Workers' Educational Association, local government, colleges, business interest and others - and in other cases they are branch organisations of I.C.O.M. In a few areas where there is a local political commitment (the London Boroughs of Wandsworth and Lambeth are examples) the Local Authority has appointed an officer with a special remit to promote and support the growth of co-operatives.

In 1978 the (Labour) Government honoured its pledge to

create a national Co-operative Development Agency. Although disappointingly restricted to advice, research, information and education (rather than the distribution of funds), it represents some commitment by Parliament to the development of a stronger co-operative sector in the British economy. The Inner Urban Areas Act of 1978 has also empowered Local Authorities in certain areas to make small loans or grants to people intending to set up co-operatives. At the same time there are discernible signs that some members and officials of the traditional co-operative movement are keen to see a move back towards the ideals and intentions which originally inspired that movement.

The development of this network of support organisations should ensure a steady growth of worker co-operatives and ensure that some of the mistakes of the last century are not repeated. It is vital, however, that political and ideological argument over details does not obscure the main aim, which is simply that people should be allowed much more control over their working lives.

Note: In our summary of British co-operative history, we have quoted freely from Richard Fletcher's contribution to *'The New Worker Co-operatives'*. (See Appendix G).

II. THE MECHANICS OF WORKERS' CO-OPERATIVES

1. What are the principles of a workers' co-operative?

A workers' co-operative has been defined as an enterprise which is 'owned and controlled by all those working in it', but we think it may be appropriate to differentiate to some extent between **ownership** and **control**. It is sometimes argued that control is impossible without ownership, but complete ownership by the workforce of the assets of a co-operative enterprise right from the start may be difficult to arrange, and insistence on it may prevent or unnecessarily delay the formation of such an enterprise.

We suggest, therefore that the basic principle of a workers' co-operative is that its management, objectives, and the use of its assets are controlled by the workforce and that complete ownership of its assets by the workforce is agreed as an **essential aim**, to be achieved as soon as possible.

Certain other principles which stem from this basic principle have come to be regarded as appropriate to a workers' co-operative and as differentiating it from other forms of 'industrial democracy'.

To enable the workforce to control the enterprise some kind of voting system will be needed, and it is considered appropriate that each member of the workforce shall have only one vote and that a majority or some higher proportion of the votes shall be decisive.

In a workers' co-operative a clear distinction should be drawn between reward for capital and reward for labour. Those who provide capital should receive a fair reward for doing so in the form of interest at an agreed rate, but any trading surplus which remains after the payment of this interest is regarded as having been created by the efforts of the workforce. It should therefore be regarded as a reward for these efforts, to be used as the workforce decide and not for the further reward of those who provide the capital. In traditional terms, loan stock is permissible but ordinary stock is not, and this principle is often expressed as 'labour hires capital, capital does not hire labour'.

Control can hardly be said to lie with the workforce if it is possible for the enterprise to be 'sold up' without their consent, and it is therefore customary to stipulate that, whatever the form of ownership structure, the enterprise cannot be dissolved except with the consent of the members and that even then the assets realised shall not be distributed to the members. This is to prevent the members at any particular time cashing in, for their own benefit, assets which have been built up by the efforts of their predecessors in the enterprise and which should be handed on for others in the future.

Not all existing co-operatives conform to all these principles. Some have a system of differential shareholdings depending on length of membership and earnings, with voting powers depending on the amount of shareholding, and there are varying degrees of control by the workforce. In fact there are as many different systems as there are co-operatives, but we think the desirable principles are as described above, and would summarise them as follows:

1. The basic principle is that the enterprise, its management, objectives and the use of its assets shall be controlled by the workforce.
2. In any system of voting, 'one man, one vote' shall apply.
3. Labour hires capital, capital does not hire labour.
4. If the workforce decide to dissolve the enterprise, they shall not benefit financially by doing so.

2. Who can start a workers' co-operative?

Anyone can start a workers' co-operative. Founders may have widely different motivations and abilities, and there is no single set of appropriate qualifications.
Some possible starting points might be:

1. **A group of workers** decide to set up in business on their own and think a co-operative would be appropriate. They may not be currently employed, may have the same or different skills, may have a recognised leader, and they may or may not be experienced in office work, accounting, sales, design, law, etc.

2. **An individual** wants to start an enterprise and thinks a co-operative would be appropriate. He may have other workers associated with him or may need to recruit them. He may believe that such a structure will be more efficient commercially or worthwhile in terms of job satisfaction. On the other hand, his motivation may be principally to demonstrate a political philosophy. Alternatively, he may have a desire to alleviate unemployment.

3. **A business** is closed down and the workforce, probably including middle management, are unwilling to accept the redundancy that faces them; the formation of a workers' co-operative may be proposed.

4. **An organisation** such as a Regional, County or District Authority, a Community or Parish Council, or some form of community organisation or Tenants' Association may wish to alleviate unemployment and/or provide some form of service to the community which is lacking, and may consider a workers' co-operative appropriate. The Job Creation Programme between 1975 and 1978 encouraged organisations such as local authorities and community groups to experiment with new forms of enterprise on co-operative lines.

5. **The shareholders** of an existing company may be willing to give or sell the company's assets to the employees.

3. What might a workers' co-operative do ?

There is no limit to the type of activity in which a co-operative might become engaged. In general it is not what is done which is the most important factor, but who does it and how it is done. A committed group with an understanding of co-operation and business sense are more likely to succeed than a disjointed group who may have a brilliant idea but who lack judgement and the ability to co-operate with one another.

In most areas of the country there are plenty of goods and services to be made and given. New firms are constantly setting up (and failing!) as people break out on their own or follow up an idea, perhaps started in their spare time. It is not the idea which makes the co-operative but the people.

It is generally easier to start up in the service sector rather than in manufacturing. Less capital is usually required, it should be fairly clear whether the service is wanted, and provided the necessary skills are available it should be possible to create a co-operative to offer it. To manufacture a product which will sell competitively will usually require a considerable period of research and development and a more thorough-going market examination. Also the capital required to set up a production line and marketing system will usually be greater.

A co-operative requires an admixture of people who have a viable idea, the ability to make the product or service and to market it, and the idealism to work as a co-operative. It is essential initially to carry out a thorough feasability study, which will examine all these factors and indicate whether the total package can be financially and co-operatively viable.

In Scotland an attempt has been made to marry together people with ideas, skills and co-operative idealism through a Register of Talents which is being compiled by means of a series of newspaper advertisements and meetings throughout the country. Local Co-operative Development Groups will clearly have an important role to play in forging links between individuals and ideas in order to create viable co-operative enterprises. In particular they should be alert to the opportunities for budding co-operatives to tap into the sources of ready-made ideas which exist in large established enterprises. It is a fact that many of these companies are seeking ways of cushioning the effect on their employees of 'rationalisation' induced by the advent of micro-processor technology and they may be glad to hive off small but viable parts of their operations.

Although there may be cases, (for example Category 4 of Section 2) where an existing organisation may be willing to some extent to subsidise an enterprise because of the beneficial effect it may have in the community, in general a co-operative is subject to the same economic forces as any other commercial enterprise.

It cannot be too strongly stressed that commercial viability is essential if a co-operative is to be credible in seeking support from external agencies, and that the paramount importance of viability will probably dictate the product or service which the enterprise provides. Enthusiasm for the co-operative idea should not be allowed to mask the need for a saleable product or service.

Many enterprises fail because insufficient thought is given to the choice of a product or service which is saleable at an economic price and which stands a fair chance of remaining so in the face of competition and forces outwith the enterprise's control. It should not be assumed that it is always necessary to mount an elaborate and costly market research exercise; on the other hand no enterprise should start without adequate thought being given to the long-term prospects. It may be helpful to make three points which, although they may appear obvious, do sometimes seem to be overlooked by co-operatives.

First, the sales of anything which could be regarded as a luxury product are liable to decrease if real incomes are decreasing. Therefore thought should be given to the possibility of producing essential goods, import substitutes and exports.

Second, there is a natural tendency for small enterprises to think in terms of sub-contract work because it lessens the need for design and active selling. We do not mean to belittle these advantages, which are considerable for a small concern, but reliance on sub-contract work does mean that the fortunes of the enterprise are more or less controlled by factors over which it has no control. There are examples of co-operatives whose viability and continued existence have been seriously threatened, and which in some cases have been put out of business, by the withdrawal of promised sub-contract work.

The third point concerns those enterprises described in Category 3 of Section 2, where the workforce of an existing company is threatened by redundancy due, perhaps, to the dissolution of the company or the transfer of its operations to another area. If in such a situation it is clear that the threatened redundancy is the result of mismanagement, or asset stripping or some other factor connected solely with the convenience of the group or of the parent company, there may be a case for continuing production of the existing product, possibly by means of a workers' co-operative. It may be, however, that the market for the product has declined to such an extent that it is no longer possible to sell it and it must therefore be changed, or that other forces are at work which make trading difficult. In such circumstances the idea that the formation of a workers' co-operative will solve the problems of the existing company should be treated with caution.

We believe that the fact that a workers' co-operative must be commercially viable needs to be emphasised. We have tried in this section to indicate some of the factors connected with choosing a product or service which must be taken into account if such viability is to be achieved. We have also stressed the importance of getting together the right mix of people. Two further factors - good organisation and management, and adequate finance - will be considered in Sections 7 and 8.

4. What commitment is required ?

Commitment, in this section, means commitment to the ideals and principles of worker co-operation. The extent to which a financial commitment by a member of a co-operative may be required or desirable will be discussed in Section 10. The motivations of prospective co-operators are diverse (the desire to relieve unemployment, to change the political system, to achieve greater job satisfaction or simply to get a larger share of the profits) and their approaches and commitment to the principles of complete worker control may therefore vary widely. We consider, however, that if a workers' co-operative is not to be merely a pseudonym of 'profit-sharing', 'worker directors', 'free collective bargaining' or some other form of 'industrial democracy', agreement to the principles of co-operation outlined in Section 1 is essential . It may, however, not always be realised how much this may conflict with traditional attitudes and ingrained, sometimes subconscious, modes of thought. Two examples may be helpful.

There was the man who said, 'I want to start a workers' co-operative but I want to hand it on to my son when I retire'. A group of skilled men said, 'We are willing to share the profits with all the workers but it will be our unselfishness, experience and hard work which will set up the enterprise, so why should we risk troublemakers getting their nominees voted into membership in order to wreck it?' (Certain safeguards against the fears expressed here are mentioned in Section 7).

Those attitudes learned in an essentially class conscious society and an industrial world where hierarchy is rigorously preserved do not prepare individuals very well for participation in the principles of common-ownership. Co-operatives often operate best where there is already a strong tradition of local solidarity, such as in the Basque area of Mondragon in Northern Spain. Nevertheless even here workers are required to participate in classes in co-operation in addition to the usual industrial and commercial skills.

The discussion involved in the drafting of a Preamble (see Appendix B) will be of enormous value in requiring the founder members to establish the aims of the business and the principles upon which it will be founded. Thorough discussion at this initial stage has often exposed important differences in attitude between members. Of course attitudes can change substantially with the implementation of a project and a balance needs to be kept between too much and too little time spent on discussion. However, regular meetings between members at the initial stages of a project can maintain the impetus and help to clarify the issues and will also help to build up relationships between members.

We have talked to the founder members of many workers' co-operatives, existing, proposed, and failed, and are of the opinion, on their advice, that it is unwise to proceed further with the formation of a co-operative unless and until all the founders are agreed on the overriding importance of **ultimate** control by the workforce. To do so or to agree to the dilution of this basic principle will create problems for the future, when they may be more difficult to solve.

It is sometimes argued that too great an insistence on agreement between the founder members (used here in the non-legal sense to denote any group of people interested in starting a co-operative) is undesirable because it may delay or even prevent the start of actual trading. Obviously, in a 'redundancy' or 'work in' situation where the business has to be kept going there is some force in this argument, but it must in our view be used with caution.

The natural desire to get the enterprise off the ground quickly may cause it to be used mainly to cover up or avoid the fact that one or more of the members of the founding group has doubts about the importance of complete worker control. It is not suggested, however, that a group contemplating the formation of a workers' co-operative should be discouraged by the existence of such reservations initially. Discussions should continue in the hope that such doubts can be resolved; it sometimes happens that those who initially have reservations on this point subsequently become strong supporters of worker control.

It is important to differentiate at this stage between agreement to the principle and agreement in detail on how it is to be implemented. Implementation will be more easily achieved once mutual trust and agreement to the principle have been established and will in any case be a matter of decision and possibly revision by the workforce as the co-operative grows.

We have suggested in this section that the commitment of the founding group to the ultimate achievement of the first of the principles summarised in Section 1 is vital to the future well-being of a workers' co-operative. We have not stressed commitment to the other three principles; not because they are unimportant, but because they follow logically from the first. Nor have we mentioned the commitments which are required of those who join a co-operative after its formation. These are to some extent more a willingness to conform to, and to help operate a previously established system and they will be discussed in Section 5 and 7, together with some of the obligations of the founders once the co-operative is established.

5. What is involved in membership?

In Section 1 and 4 we suggested that control by the work-force must be the overriding principle governing the affairs of a workers' co-operative and that there should be no dilution of this principle, and in Section 3 we stressed the need for commercial viability. Does it therefore follow that if commercial viability can be reconciled with complete worker control a workers' co-operative will be a success?

Our study of existing and failed co-operatives leads us to believe that it does, and that what is involved in membership is largely a willingness and determination to achieve this reconciliation, but its achievement is not easy and presents certain problems. Section 7 indicates some of the ways in which the structure of a co-operative may have to differ from a traditional structure in order to overcome these problems. Section 5 describes a basic difficulty which seems to beset most co-operatives in their early years and which can usefully be considered in two parts involving two groups of people, one of which comprises those who in a traditional system might be called the 'management', and the other which comprises the 'workers'.

1. Entrepreneurial skill is usually essential in the early stages of a commercially successful enterprise, and those who possess it often do not take kindly to discussing their ideas or intended actions with others, particularly a committee, and may find it difficult to operate effectively if they have to do so. The same is true to some extent of organising skill and expertise in some complex technical field. If a spirit of trust is to develop in a co-operative, people with such skills should be at pains to explain their actions and intentions to their fellow members whenever possible. The need for commercial secrecy can sometimes be used as an excuse for unnecessary reticence.

2. In any average workforce there are likely to be a number of people who though they may wish to participate in making decisions have no experience of doing so, especially via a committee/voting system. They need time to overcome their reticence and gain confidence both in themselves and the system before they feel able to contribute. If such a system is expected to work too early in the life of a co-operative, two results are likely. First, wrong or half-hearted decisions may be taken at a time when they can be least afforded. Second, the workforce as a whole is likely to lose faith in the system and either drift away or demand a more traditional form of management structure, thereby forfeiting the very real benefits worker control can produce.

What is needed is time for learning and adjustment of attitudes by both the groups described above, and this need is most likely to be in evidence in the areas of high unemployment which are currently proving a fruitful field for the establishment of co-operatives; areas where the workforce may tend to lack managerial and participative experience and skill. Meanwhile the enterprise has to be started or, in a redundancy situation, kept going, and the closing paragraphs of this section offer some suggestions on how this may more easily be achieved.

Training programmes arranged in liaison with a local business school or resource body have been used to good effect. Also, in the early years, some modification of total control by the workforce might well be allowed and agreed. We are aware that this idea will be regarded as heresy in some quarters on the grounds that it represents 'dilution', but note that in Section 4 we suggested that it is the principle of **ultimate** control which should not be diluted. There is, however, evidence that those co-operatives that have adopted this approach (it is sometimes referred to as a 'Pre-Co-op' system) have eventually been more successful, both commercially and ideologically, than some of those which have tried to use a 'total democracy, total consultation' system from the start.

While there is considerable merit in this idea of working **towards** full control by the whole workforce there is of course a danger inherent in it, namely that the founders, or 'management' may ultimately not be willing to relinquish control completely, which is why, again in Section 4, we stressed the need for the founders' agreement to this principle before the enterprise is allowed to start. It may therefore be wise to indicate in the registration documents the intention that complete worker control shall operate as soon as all concerned agree that it can do so effectively, both in terms of commercial viability and of commitment by a substantial part of the workforce.

It has been wisely said by someone with a great deal of experience of this type of enterprise, 'Perhaps every workers' co-operative needs its autocrats initially, but will only really have succeeded when it has got rid of them'. Strong, but nonetheless practical advice. In a well run co-operative the autocrats will hopefully have been absorbed into the enterprise or have left to start new co-operatives. What they must not try, or be allowed, to do is to remain as autocrats within the enterprise.

6. Why is a legal structure desirable and what form of legal structure is most appropriate ?

As soon as the members of a founding group feel that they are sufficiently agreed on their intentions, they will be wise to seek legal registration or incorporation, because:

1. The enterprise is then likely to have more credibility with those with whom it trades or from whom it seeks assistance (financial or advisory).
2. The members of the enterprise will then have limited liability, so that their personal assets will not be at risk.
3. Some form of 'constitution' will be required as part of the process of acquiring legal status, and the process of decid-

ing on this should be useful in further crystallising the objectives of the enterprise as a framework within which
to take decisions in the future.
4. No enterprise has to obtain a certificate under the Industrial Common Ownership(ICO)Act, 1976 but such a certificate may confer certain benefits. A formal legal structure,
   either under the Companies Acts or the Industrial and Provident Societies Acts, will facilitate recognition under
   the ICO Act (see Appendix D).

Four types of legal structure can be used by enterprises:
   i) A Partnership
   ii) A Company Limited by Shares
   iii) A Registered Society under the Industrial and Pro-
        vident Societies Acts (a Registered Co-operative).
   iv) A Company Limited by Guarantee without Share Capital.

The suitability of each type to a workers' co-operative is considered below, the criterion being how readily each type can
be made to incorporate the principles suggested in Part II,
Section 1 of this handbook.

i) Formation of a Partnership under the Partnership Act.
A group of people working together in a business which has
no legal structure constitutes a partnership for legal and tax
purposes, whether or not written partnership agreements have
been made, and a partnership can consist of up to 20 people,
but the partners cannot have limited liability. The first three
of our four principles can be fulfilled by a partnership provided
that all the workers are partners, but the business may be sold
for the benefit of the workforce.

Groups of less than seven people wishing to form a co-
operative may use this structure and then convert to a Registered Co-operative (see iii below) when their numbers reach
seven. This would give them the advantage of being able to
form the co-operative with less than seven members without
introducing non-working members. The use of this type of
structure is not recommended in the long term and is not
recommended at all for groups of seven or more members.

ii) Incorporation as a Company Limited by Shares under the
Companies Acts. This type of legal structure is the one adop-

ted by what most people think of as a 'company'. Its principal intentions are to enable those who buy its shares, who are often not members of its workforce, to control the company and benefit from its financial success. It usually provides that votes shall be in proportion to capital invested and that dividends to shareholders shall be at least partially related to the success and profits of the company. It also enables the shareholders to dissolve the company and share in the proceeds of doing so.

Reference to Part II, Section 1 of this handbook will show that these intentions run counter to all the generally accepted principles of a workers' co-operative and although in theory and at great trouble and expense, a Memorandum and Articles of Association which might get round these difficulties could be drafted, there seems little point in attempting to do so when two other structures are available which are much more adaptable to the needs of a workers' co-operative. These are described below.

iii) Registration as a Co-operative Society under the Industrial and Provident Societies (I & PS) Acts, 1965-75. Whereas companies limited by shares are basically concerned with the interests of outside shareholders, the I & PS Acts embody the experience over some hundred years of enterprises designed to be controlled by members involved in the enterprise.

The I & PS Act, 1965 is the principal Act, and the most important parts of it, as far as the non-lawyer is concerned, are Section 1 and Schedule 1.

Section 1 of the Act states that any enterprise which wishes to be registered under the Act must, except in special circumstances, be a bona fide co-operative society. Some discretion as to what constitues a bona fide co-operative society is allowed to the Registrar of Friendly Societies who administers the I & PS Acts, but guidance on this point is available because Section 1 also lays down that a registered co-operative must have Rules and Schedule 1 states what must be included in these Rules. Additionally, Form F 617 (see Appendix C) describes in layman's language the main conditions which a bona fide co-operative society must satisfy. The special circumstances described in Paragraphs 3 and 4 of Form F 617 are unlikely to apply to the type of enterprise for which this handbook has been written.

All the legal structures discussed in this section require the drafting of some form of 'constitution' to regulate and formalise the conduct of the affairs of the enterprise, and it is the Rules which fulfil this function under the I & PS Acts. Application for registration will probably be more quickly and easily achieved if application is made through a 'promoting body' recognised by the Registrar, using Model Rules. The Co-operative Union and the Industrial Common Ownership Movement (ICOM) (see Appendix A) are recognised promoting bodies.

ICOM Model Rules embody the principles set out in Part II, Section 1 of this handbook, i.e. control by the working members (Rules 6 - 8, 10) 'one man, one vote' (Rule 11), no dissolution for personal profit (Rule 18) and the concept of a share as a 'membership ticket' rather than as a dividend-earning financial stake in the enterprise (Rule 5). The procedure for registration through ICOM is summarised in Appendix B, which also contains a copy of its Model Rules.

iv) Incorporation as a Company Limited by Guarantee without Share Capital under the Companies Acts. This type of legal structure has not traditionally been used by industrial enterprises but there is no reason why it should not be used by a workers' co-operative, particularly in a 'group' or 'change-over' situation (see below) or if more flexibility in the 'constitution' is desired than is permitted by the I & PS Acts.

At least two ICOM companies have used this type of legal structure. ICOM is in the process of drafting a model constitution for this type of legal structure which will enable simple registration and compliance with the ICO Act.

A summary of the relative advantages and disavantages of the two structures, Registration as a Society under the I & PS Acts and Incorporation as a Company Limited by Guarantee without Share Capital, follows:

a. Registration fees for Model Rules under the I & PS Acts (£42 plus £20 for Associate Membership of ICOM, if ICOM is the promoting body) are less than incorporation fees under the Companies Acts (£50 to which must be added the cost of the Memorandum and Articles of Association). Also Annual Returns, which involve the filing of audited accounts with the appropriate Registrar, cost less for registered co-operatives. A Company pays £20 p.a., but there is no charge for a registered co-operative.

b. In the case of a 'hybrid' constitution (i.e. when Model Rules are not used) the application procedure is likely to be cheaper under the I & PS Acts because the Registrar of Friendly Societies is prepared to advise on procedural matters, whereas the Registrar of Companies tends to refer enquiries to a solicitor. In either case time and money can be saved by obtaining copies of constitutions from similar organisations to the one which is being set up. It may well be possible to create a constitution for the new co-operative by copying an existing constitution or slightly amending it, using the services of the Registrar of Friendly Societies or a solicitor if necessary. Copies of constitutions may be obtained from the organisations themselves, (Registered Co-operatives are required to provide copies for a maximum of 10p), or from the appropriate Registrar by using the public search facilities.

c. Corporation Tax is 40% under the I & PS Acts compared with between 42% and 52%, depending on the amount of profits, under the Companies Acts (as at April 1979).

d. Although registration under the I & PS Acts creates, strictly speaking, a Society, such Societies are generally regarded as, and called, Co-operatives by the public and the media. We shall therefore use the title 'Registered Co-operative' in the remainder this section. Some enterprises, however, although operating on co-operative principles, may wish to avoid the image created by the title 'Co-operative' which is sometimes found to be commercially unhelpful. Also, the I & PS Acts permit the issue of shares, and although their importance can be reduced by making them merely a 'membership ticket' as in the ICOM Model Rules, shares are associated by most people with 'weighted' voting and dividends. These difficulties do not arise in a Company Limited by Guarantee without Share Capital.

e. A Registered Co-operative must always have at least seven members, but two can form a Company. This means that if a group with less than seven members wished to form a Registered Co-operative, the seven founder members could not all be workers; some of them would have to be 'outsiders' or non-working members. Such 'outsiders' should normally be asked to resign when the size of the co-operative reaches seven working members, but because this procedure cannot be arranged automatically in the Rules, it is a potentially undesirable situation (but see Part II, Section 5 about the 'Pre-Co-op' system).The ICOM model rules contain an interesting solution to this problem (rule 6(a)) in that 'outsiders' normally have to resign when an ICO Act certificate is applied for.

f. A Registered Co-operative cannot have charitable status. Charitable status can confer certain tax advantages but this status is unlikely to be granted to an enterprise which exists to benefit its members financially and this point is therefore unlikely to be important as far as most workers' co-operatives are concerned.

g. A Company with less than eleven members may be regarded by the Inland Revenue as a close company. This can result in certain types of expenditure being disallowed for tax purposes and in liability to both corporation tax and income tax. This difficulty cannot arise in the case of a Registered Co-operative, which cannot also be a close company.

h. The rate of interest payable on borrowed capital may be limited in the case of a Registered Co-operative by its Rules or by the Registrar, but this restriction need not apply to a Company. A Company may thus find it easier to attract capital.

i. The 'group' situation. Where it is intended that a 'parent' organisation shall provide central services, and possibly loan finance, to a number of independent workers' co-operatives the I & PS Acts would probably be found to be too restrictive to provide a suitable structure for the 'parent' organisation. A Company Limited by Guarantee without Share Capital might be more appropriate.

However, where it is proposed to found a group of co-operatives with centralised services it is possible to use the Registered Co-operative legal structure as the umbrella organisation. Each sub-group co-operative then need not have its own legal identity but instead can be a 'division' of the main co-operative. When any sub-group reaches financial maturity the decision can be made whether or not to make that sub-group a separate legal entity (i.e. a Registered Co-operative).

j. The 'changeover' situation. This is the situation described in Part II, Section 2, Category 5 of this handbook, where it is intended to change a 'traditional' company, limited by shares, into a workers' co-operative. Some of the considerations involved are outlined below.

The simplest method is to change the Company into a Registered Co-operative under the provisions of the I & PS Act 1965, Section 53. (see also I & PS Acts 1967 and 1975).

Alternatively, the shareholders of the existing Company may sell or give their shares to a Company Limited by Guarantee without Share Capital (the workers' co-operative). The existing company continues to trade but is controlled by the workers' co-operative which now holds all its shares.

Alternatively, and more simply, the existing company sells or gives all its assets to a Company Limited by Guarantee without Share Capital (the workers' co-operative). The existing company then ceases to trade and the workers' co-operative takes over its operations.

In any changeover situation liability to Capital Transfer Tax (CTT) and Capital Gains Tax (CGT) is likely to arise. If an 'employee trust' (as defined by paragraph 17 of Schedule 5 of the Finance Act 1975) is set up to act as a vehicle for the changeover then much of the tax liability may be avoided.

For a full discussion of the tax implications of changeover see: **'Common Ownership and Co-operative Enterprises and Taxation'** available free of charge from the Department of Industry. For full details of the use of an 'employee trust' and other useful information about changeover see: **'How to convert a company into an industrial co-operative'** by R.D. Sawtell (see Appendix G).

Summary

This section of the handbook shows that there can be no hard and fast rules as to the best legal structure for any particular workers' co-operative. It emphasises the need for such a structure and sets out the pros and cons, from a co-operative point of view, of each type of structure. Partnerships and Companies Limited by Shares, because of their emphasis on personal, rather than corporate, gain can only be adapted with great diffuculty to the principles of worker co-operation. Small enterprises starting from scratch may well feel that the tailor made nature of a Registered Co-operative under the Industrial and Provident Societies Acts, with Model Rules, suits their needs. If more flexibility is required Model Rules can be modified or the advantages of a Company Limited by Guarantee without Share Capital can be investigated. The latter structure may well have distinct advantages for larger enterprises and in complex legal situations.

A word of warning on the possible costs of forming a suitable Company Limited by Guarantee without Share Capital may be appropriate. Registration under the I & PS Acts can be quickly and cheaply accomplished with the help of the Registrar and a promoting body, but forming a Company will require the services of a lawyer. Work is currently in hand on the drafting of a Model Memorandum and Articles of Association and this should greatly cheapen the process of forming a 'Co-operative Company', but meantime there are few lawyers with relevant knowledge or experience and unless a suitable lawyer is chosen much money can be spent to little effect.

7. How is a workers' co-operative organised ?

The word 'organised' is used here in its widest sense and in this section we have tried to gather up problems connected with the functioning of workers' co-operatives which have emerged from our enquiries and which have not been discussed in other sections. It is not intended to be a guide to the organisation of commercial enterprises in general, but to highlight some of the problems which are more or less exclusive to workers' co-operatives and to comment upon them. We shall refer to the ICOM Model Rules from time to time in this section, not because they are by any means the only constitution which a workers' co-operative can adopt, and in any case can be modified, but because they embody the principles outlined in Section 1, and are a useful framework in which to set our comments.

Who are the members of a workers' co-operative?

In general, a 'member' is anyone who shares in the control of the co-operative, and under the ICOM Model Rules membership is confined to those who are in the employment of the co-operative plus the founder members (who need not be in the employment of the co-operative unless a certificate under the ICO Act is sought, in which case those not in employment would cease to be members - see rule 6(b)). Under those rules voting is confined to members, who have one vote each.

Are all the workers in a co-operative members?

Most co-operatives specify a lower age limit and most do not require that every worker shall become a member. Sometimes up to 30% of the workforce does not apply for membership. Under the ICO Act at least 50% of employees must be members.

In some co-operatives, everyone is offered immediate formal membership, and therefore immediate voting rights, but in many others this system does not operate. Its dangers are twofold.

First, people who are apathetic to the co-operative aspects of the enterprise but who could, given time, become interested in them and contribute to their development, (see Section 5), may be given voting rights too early and through apathy or ill-considered use of their votes, may bring about a general disillusion with the principles of co-operation which may eventually lead to the complete neglect of these principles. Second, some people may disagree with the whole idea of workers' co-operatives on the grounds that their members are exploiting their fellow workers or themselves or both, or that they are merely a variant of the capitalist system, which they would prefer to see dismantled or destroyed. If employment gives automatic voting membership, the membership could be 'packed' with people of this persuasion, and control could fall into their hands. This may seem far-fetched but we know of a group of workers who gave much thought to the starting of a co-operative, and the fear of such a take-over was one of the reasons why they did not do so, in spite of the possible safeguards suggested in the next few paragraphs, which were explained to them. A further hazard is the temptation and pressure in a competitive environment to employ people for their skills alone and to disregard their interest in co-operation, which may be nil. If many such people are permitted membership, the neglect of co-operative principles mentioned above is likely to occur.

What conditions of membership can, or should be imposed?

The short answer to both these questions in a democratic system must be none, except the acceptance of new members by the existing members, as shown by vote. This view is supported by the ICOM Model Rules and the ICO Act. Neither document, however, says that the existing membership may not impose conditions on itself as to who may be accepted and when, and both documents mention this possibility.

Principally as a safeguard against the dangers described

above, many co-operatives have a probationary system. Under this no worker may become a member until he or she has worked in the enterprise for a certain period (typically 3 - 18 months) so that the existing members, who are of course all workers who have gone through the same process, may have sufficient opportunity to judge whether or not a candidate for membership will be an asset to the co-operative as a voting (controlling) member. A probationary period will also give a new employee time to decide whether, in fact, he wants to become a member.

Such a system seems to have much to commend it, but it is essential that it is the workforce as a whole, not the 'management', which ultimately takes decisions on a person's suitability for membership. It should also be recognised that the probationary system can give rise to tensions between members, non-members and aspiring members.

What pay structure is appropriate?
The co-operative ideal is that skill, experience, responsibility, etc. should not be rewarded by different rates of pay, because if everyone is contributing to the maximum of his or her ability differentials are inappropriate and unfair.

Admirable as this concept of equality of effort and reward may be, it is for many reasons difficult to achieve in practice. For example, it requires a degree of commitment to co-operative ideals which is unlikely to be shared by the whole workforce, different needs dictated by different personal circumstances might reasonably be taken into account, and it is contrary to the current attitudes of most workers in this country and to the current attitudes of most Trade Unions.

In practice most co-operatives take account of such facts of industrial life and operate some sort of compromise between zero differentials and the wide differential ratios which obtain in many traditional companies by limiting this ratio. Our enquiries indicate, however, that whether or not a co-operative is a union shop, union rates and the need to compete for labour tend to dictate pay rates if the enterprise is to be viable commercially. What is important, and different, about a co-operative enterprise is that the forces dictating rates of pay are, or should be, explained to and discussed by the whole workforce, who must be the people who ultimately decide what rates are paid.

What about overtime and redundancies?

The original reason for the payment of higher rates for hours worked outside the normal working period was that people did not want to work outside this period and so should be compensated for having to do so, but in many industries overtime working and payment for it have now become an essential part of the wages structure. This obviously conflicts with one of the aims of co-operatives, which is to provide better working conditions including a reasonable amount of leisure time, and some co-operatives have a system of time off in lieu of extra payment when work outside normal hours is unavoidable.

One of the objectives of workers' co-operatives is to provide greater job security, and particularly to avoid the sudden and inadequately explained pay-offs which are a feature of some traditionally organised enterprises. Some co-operatives aim at the ideal of no redundancies, but there can be a conflict between this ideal and the need for commercial viability. If the market reduces it may be advisable for commercial reasons to reduce expenditure on wages, and if a change in the market dictates a change in the skills required it may then be difficult to find suitable jobs within the enterprise for those whose skills are no longer relevant. In this situation the unpleasant decision as to whether to pay off long-standing, possibly founding, members may have to be faced.

There are no easy solutions to these problems, but obviously a thorough examination must be made of ways of reducing expenditure other than redundancy and such measures as job sharing and short time working can be explored. What is important in a co-operative is that the workforce as a whole, not the 'management', decide how they are to be solved.

How does worker control operate, and does it conflict with efficient management?

There are almost as many answers to the first part of this question as there are co-operatives, but in most co-operatives there is some sort of works committee whose functions, powers and frequency of meeting depend on the extent to which complete worker control is operating (see Section 5).

In a small enterprise this committee may consist of the whole workforce,meeting perhaps weekly, but as the enterprise grows this system is likely to become impracticable for reasons of size and because it is unlikely that all the members of the workforce will be willing or able to meet so frequently. A system whereby a Works, or Management, Committee is elected by a General Meeting may therefore evolve, and Sub-Committees may be appointed to deal with such matters as pay differentials, long term plans and the purely co-operative aspects of the enterprise.

There is obviously a danger that as the co-operative gets larger and the system more elaborate a feeling of disinterest and remoteness from power may grow, and some co-operatives see this as a reason for deliberately limiting their size; others make a special point of recognising this tendency and trying to prevent its adverse effects, sometimes by appointing 'trustees' from outwith the company whose task is to act as arbiters when difficult decisions must be taken and to keep a watching brief on the co-operative aspects of the enterpise. The division of the enterprise into small semi-autonomous work units has also been found to be helpful in preserving a sense of commitment and 'belonging'.

It is sometimes argued that complete worker-control is incompatible with any sort of line structure or management. However, except in some of the smallest of co-operatives, the application of this philosophy in practice, in the sense that no-one is answerable to anyone, no-one takes decisions which may affect others, and all decisions, no matter how small, must be discussed in detail by all members before they are taken, is not found to lead either to increased job satisfaction or to commercial viability.

The function of management in any well run enterprise

can, at the risk of some oversimplification, be expressed as follows. Someone needs to allocate tasks from day to day and generally co-ordinate the work at the point of production, whether on the factory floor, or elsewhere as in a building or plant hire business; someone needs to deal with secretarial work, accounts, VAT, etc.; someone needs to think ahead, order materials and keep an eye on finance and cash-flow; a sales/marketing person may be needed; and so may a design/research person. So often when a group of hard working people, highly skilled and experienced in their trade(s) decide to set up in business it is the lack of an appreciation of the need for these functions and what is involved in them, (they can be left to somebody's wife, part-time and unpaid), that brings the business to its knees. It is unrealistic and commercially dangerous to think that a co-operative system will remove the need for these functions, but if such a system is generating the trust and willingness to 'muck in' which is evident in successful co-operatives, the task of those responsible for carrying out these functions may well be easier and more rewarding than in a traditional enterprise.

How should management be provided in a workers' co-operative?

There are three basic options. First and ideally, the people who do 'management' jobs will be elected to do them by a vote of the whole workforce or by a sub-committee of the workforce. Second, if by general agreement some control is still retained by the founding group, it may be agreed that one or more of that group, though not formal members of the co-operative, shall be responsible for one or more of these jobs, and in the early years of a co-operative where there is goodwill and common sense the workforce sometimes prefer this arrangement. Third, management can be hired; i.e. people with the appropriate skills not possessed by the members, who are not members of the co-operative and who do not wish to become so, are employed by the co-operative to manage the commercial, but **not** the co-operative aspects of its affairs. The concept here is that management is simply a skill, like welding or draughtsmanship, and does not denote rank in a hierarchy, nor the right to power except in so far as it is delegated to the manager by the workforce. In existing co-operatives these three ways of providing management services often occur in some sort of combination with one another, and which of them is used, and to what extent, depends on all sorts of factors, such as the commitment of the workforce and the founders to worker control and the extent to which it operates, the complexity of the business and the skills possessed by the members, and it is therefore neither possible nor useful to try to lay down hard and fast rules. We shall therefore confine ourselves to an outline of some of the factors which may influence a choice.

If the basic principle of a workers's co-operative is the achievement of full control by the members as quickly as possible it seems desirable that the necessary management positions should be filled from among the members as soon as possible, but it may be unwise to pursue this ideal too enthusiastically without taking the following factors into account. First, the necessary skills may not be available in the membership and no enterprise can afford much amateur management in its early stages. Second, there is the possibility that people may be elected who, though popular or with strong personalities, may lack the necessary tact or firmness to get things done willingly and efficiently. Third, time may be required for commitment and trust to develop before members are willing to participate fully in a voting system, whether as electors or candidates for management type jobs, as suggested in Section 5.

Because of these factors it may be decided that one of the other two options or a combination of them with the first, should be adopted, i.e. some management should be performed by one or more of the founders although he or she is not a full member, or by hired management.

In either case the important thing would seem to be that any manager thus appointed recognises that his powers, particularly where long-term objectives and co-operative matters are concerned, are subject to the control of the membership. There is a tendency in practice for managers to pursue efficiency and profits to the exclusion of co-operative principles, and this needs to be guarded against. One of their tasks in a workers' co-operative, unless it is decided to employ hired management permanently, may be to work themselves out of a job by fostering co-operation and encouraging members of the workforce to assume management responsibilities.

8. What finance does a workers' co-operative need ?

In this section we shall consider why a co-operative needs money and the need for care and advice in deciding how best to use it, and we shall look briefly at some sources of finance for a workers' co-operative. In Appendix A we give the names and addresses of the main agencies which can help co-operatives to obtain funds.

It is unwise to believe that the need for finance and the efficient use if it will be any less in a co-operative than in a traditional enterprise. Both need adequate capital, finance to purchase everything that is needed to commence operating and money to pay wages and other costs until sales can produce an adequate income.

It may be prudent to regard co-operative principles, especially if they are intended to operate from the outset, as a complication added to the usual problems of starting a business. The difficulties of reconciling co-operative ideals with efficient organisation can cause short-sighted financial decisions to be taken. It should also be recognised that in some quarters where finance may be sought, the word 'co-operative' and the concept of self-management are not highly regarded. Any founding group should include or get advice from someone with proven financial ability and judgement, not necessarily someone with formal accountancy qualifications, but someone who for example has actually started and run a business or has experience in putting together successful business packages.

In any event the founding group must draw up a detailed budget and financial projections for their proposed enterprise, together with a summary of the production and marketing strategy and information about the legal structure of the enterprise, its history and its founder members. This will be the business portfolio which will be presented to potential suppliers of finance. Producing such a portfolio will be found to concentrate the mind wonderfully, in that the founders must think through each aspect of their plans and consider various contingencies. The final plan and projections can be used as a yardstick against which to measure actual performance once trading has started. In Appendix E we give an example of a budget (with notes) which is the very minimum which the founders of an enterprise should put together. In Appendix F we reproduce parts of leaflets published by Industrial Common Ownership Finance Limited and one of these outlines the type of information required by that organisation from an applicant enterprise.

While many of the official agencies listed in Appendix A can give some advice about finance they are seldom able to assist with the detailed work of putting together a business portfolio. Occasionally local authorities have advisers who are willing to help with such work and many areas are now served by local Co-operative Development Groups or by Local Enterprise Trusts. Even where such organisations exist, prospective co-operators should make a point of seeking the advice of local business people and technical and commercial colleges.

There is no special source of finance for workers' co-operatives; indeed, because of the connotations associated with the word 'co-operative' already mentioned, it is sometimes harder for co-operatives to raise capital than it is for traditionally structured businesses.

Having calculated how much capital is required, the founding members will need to explore all possible sources of finance. The following is a list of the major potential sources of finance for co-operatives:

a. Members' own resources: How much can the members themselves provide in cash, by credit or by loan guarantee? If nothing immediately, could members make a contribution out of wages during the first few years?

b. Capital from private sources: Is it possible to borrow from friends or relatives? (But beware of spoiling hitherto friendly relationships by introducing financial obligations. The effect on such relationships of failing to honour commitments can be disastrous. Make a proper and clear arrangement). Are there links with local organisations such as churches or trade unions which might provide loans or grants?

c. Bank loans: Approach the local bank manager for an overdraft or for a loan. He will certainly require a well thought out plan and a good presentation and will almost certainly demand that there is a percentage of members' contributions. If you fail with one bank, try another and another. Even different branches of the same bank might react to you and your plans in different ways.

d. Deferred payments: Don't pay for things until you have to. Can you get materials on credit? Can you hire or lease equipment and machinery, or buy it on hire purchase? (But beware of high interest rates sometimes concealed in such arrangements).

e. Government assistance: Find out what assistance you might be entitled to by contacting the Department of Industry or your Local Authority. Some Local Authorities have their own small loans schemes.

f. Special local arrangements: In some areas there are local trusts or funds which might help co-operative projects. District or Parish Councils should have information.

g. Industrial Common Ownership Finance Ltd: ICOF is a loan fund set up especially for workers' co-operatives. Its funds come from Government, from private sources and from profitable co-operative businesses.

9. How do co-operative principles affect the financial structure of a workers' co-operative?

The word 'profit' has different meanings in different contexts. In this and subsequent sections it means money available for distribution after all operating expenses, including payment of interest on borrowed money but not the transfer of any money to reserve, have been paid.

In Section 1 we suggested four principles by which a workers' co-operative should be bound, namely control by the workforce, 'one man, one vote', no participation in the profits by people outside the workforce and no dissolution for personal gain.

It is the third of these principles which is particularly important in any consideration of the financial structure of a workers' co-operative. It expresses the idea inherent in co-operative thought since the days of the Rochdale Pioneers that profits are the results of the efforts of labour i.e. of the workforce, both 'management' and 'workers' and that in fairness profits should therefore be available to the workforce to dispose of as they think fit and should not be distributed to those who provide capital. It does not imply that capital is undesirable nor does it deny that capital is entitled to a fair return. It states only that a clear distinction should be made between **capital** and **labour;** capital should receive a return which depends solely on the going rate necessary to hire it, and labour should receive the results of its own efforts, i.e. the profit.

This concept of separate rewards for separate contributions is intimately related to the choice of a suitable financial structure for a co-operative and failure to recognise and take account of this relationship has led, and continues to lead, to much confused thinking.

For example, we were talking to one of the members of a co-operative which came into existence as a result of the workforce acquiring the assets and shares of a Company Limited by Shares which had been put into liquidation by the previous shareholders. Commercial viability was, and still is, the main concern of the members of the co-operative and not surprisingly little time has been available for thought on the suitability of the original capital structure of the company from a co-operative point of view, so that it remains a Company Limited by Shares. We were told that co-operation was not working, because 'the member who has invested ten pounds regards the member who has invested two thousand pounds as his boss'. On enquiring why this should be, we were told 'because when we come to make a profit the large investor will get a dividend two hundred times more than the small investor'.

Now both of these 'investors' are members of the workforce but no differentiation is being made between the contributions each is making to the co-operative as capitalist and worker. Let us assume that £1,000 is available for distribution in a particular year before payment of interest on borrowed money. Further, let us ignore the existence of any members or lenders other than these two; to do so will not affect the point we wish to make. Under the present system the first member will get approximately £5 and the second £995. If, however, the co-operative had a capital system in accordance with the idea of the distinct contributions of capital and labour outlined earlier in this section, the picture would be very different. Assuming the going rate for borrowing to be 10% the 'low' member would receive £1 as interest on the money he had lent, and the 'high' member £200. £799 would be left as a reward for labour, and if both members were deemed to have contributed equally in terms of effort this would be split equally between them and each would receive £399.50. 'Low' would then get a total of £400.50 and 'high' would get £599.50. If a system of distribution of profit was adopted which takes account of time, skill and responsibility, as suggested in Section 10, and if 'low' was deemed to have contributed more in this respect than 'high', then their positions might even be reversed.

We have tried to show above how important it is that the

financial structure of a co-operative should be designed to give those who provide capital, whether or not they are members of the workforce, a return on their money which is independent of the financial success of the enterprise. We have also shown how the concept of shares leads to confusion in the minds of co-operators. We shall now try to show the extent to which various legal structures can be, or have been, used to accommodate the concept of separate rewards for capital and labour. In doing so, some repetition of matters already discussed in Section 6 will be unavoidable because of the close relationship which must exist between the legal and financial structures of any enterprise, and because each section is intended to be as far as possible complete in itself.

In a Company Limited by Shares the role of the Ordinary Shares tends to be dominant. They normally carry the right to vote and thus to control the company. Votes and dividends from profits are normally in proportion to the shareholdings of individuals, and the shareholders, through their votes, have the ability to dissolve the company for their personal gain. Ordinary shares are thus likely to conflict with all four of our principles and although structures involving non-voting shares, etc. can be devised, one is really fighting the system in doing so, and as we said in Section 6 this method of incorporation therefore seems basically unsuited to the principles of a workers' co-operative.

A Company Limited by Guarantee without Share Capital has the merit from a co-operative point of view of being free from the confusion often caused by the word 'shares' and a Memorandum and Articles of Association including entrenched clauses which would have the force of Rules under the Industrial and Provident Societies (I & PS)Acts, is being drafted by ICOM to include all our four principles. It would seem therefore that this method of incorporation should not be overlooked by a workers' co-operative since it may have advantages in terms of flexibility and lack of ambiguity, but a close watch must be kept on the possible legal costs involved in adopting this type of structure.

Reference to Form F 617 (see Appendix C) will show that although in general 'one man, one vote' is required by the I & PS Acts, shareholders are not required to be members of the workforce and dissolution for the benefit of the members is not excluded. All shareholders may receive dividends which depend on the financial success of the enterprise. Thus part of the profits may go to people who, according to the idea of the relationship between capital and labour set out at the start of this section, have not contributed to the making of them. Three of our principles may thus be violated unless the Rules are so written as to prevent this happening.

The ICOM Model Rules (see Appendix B) are so written. No dividends are payable on shares, which are deliberately relegated to the status of a 'membership ticket'. Dissolution for the benefit of the membership is forbidden and a very clear distinction in accordance with the ideas set out at the start of this section is made between reward for capital and reward for labour. Capital is raised and rewarded under Rules 9(a) - (c), and Rule 9(b) clearly states a rate of interest which is not dependent on profits. Rule 9(d) is not connected with the raising of capital and is a rule required by the I & PS Acts to prevent the co-operative trading primarily as a Savings Bank.

Rule 14 requires that profits shall be used either as a general reserve, or as a bonus to members, or for social and charitable purposes.

Some people argue that Companies without Share Capital or which use ICOM Model Rules (which deliberately give shares a minor, internal role) have little hope of attracting capital because they have no shares. In our view this is a misleading statement.

Organisations with the legal structures mentioned in the preceding paragraph have decided that they wish to be bound by our third principle, i.e. they are not willing to distribute their profits to outside investors. To use an analogy with a 'traditional' company, they are willing to issue Debentures but not Ordinary Shares, and not surprisingly they forfeit the attentions of a whole class of outside investors who are looking for the chance of participating in the success of the enterprise.

i.e. a say in its management, a share in its profits through dividends and the possibility of capital appreciation, all in proportion to the amount they invest. To say that a decision by such co-operatives not to issue shares reduces their chances of raising capital may be true but it seems to us to mask the basic reason underlying that decision, which is to make clear their adherence to a long-established co-operative principle.

One sometimes also hears it argued that any enterprise which does not issue shares will find it difficult to raise capital because shares are supposed to be in some way a measure of the enterprise's likelihood of success and of its possession of assets which can act as security for loans, but this argument does not seem to us to be valid. The likelihood of success depends on a number of factors - the track record of the founders, the nature of the product, etc. - none of which depend on the existence or absence of shares, and the amount of shares issued by an enterprise is no measure of its assets, as the existence of innumerable 'hundred pound companies' shows. This is so whether the enterprise is 'traditional' or co-operative. There is, of course, no question of principle involved here, only muddled thinking on the facts of commercial life.

There is no doubt that the ICOM Model Rules represent the 'purest' structure available at the present time as far as co-operative principles are concerned, but as we have pointed out above they are considerably more restrictive than the requirements of the I & PS Acts, and we shall now briefly describe some of the Rules under the I & PS Acts which are used by one of the old-established co-operatives which is a member of the Co-operative Productive Federation (see Part I). Each member has only one vote regardless of shareholding, but membership is not confined to the workforce and the only criterion for membership is approval of an application by the committee and the purchase of five £1 shares. Thus control is not confined to the workforce. Any number of shares may be held by a member up to the limit of £5,000 imposed by the I & PS Act, 1975. Interest and a dividend out of profits, the total being limited to 7½%, may be paid on shares and thus not only do people outside the workforce share in profits but profits may be distributed in proportion to capital provided rather than in proportion to labour contributed. Profits may also be distributed to customers of the co-operative and the members may dissolve the co-operative and share in the proceeds of so doing.

It is clear that although these Rules comply with the I & PS Acts they are less 'pure' in terms of our four principles, than the ICOM Model Rules. In Section 12 we shall return to the subject of 'purity'.

It is not our purpose to be dogmatic on the subject of financial and legal structures, either in this section or in Section 6. It is a well established co-operative maxim that it is the intention, rather than the method of expressing it, which is important. For instance, one of the ICOM member companies is a Company Limited by Shares but distributes its profits in proportion to wages rather than shareholding; in theory 'one man, one vote' does not apply but we are assured that this has mattered little in practice because a vote has rarely been necessary. Different structures will suit different circumstances and local Co-operative Development Groups will be able to offer advice in any particular case, (see Appendix A)

10. What happens to the profits ?

In the previous section we explained how the long-established co-operative idea of separate rewards for capital and labour implies that any money which is left after all operating costs have been met, (including the servicing of any loans, whether from members of the workforce or from outside), should be at the disposal of the workforce. Does this mean that all of this money can normally be distributed to the members of the workforce in cash?

To answer this question it will be helpful to consider three ways of using profits which are all in accordance with co-operative principles and are itemised in Rule 14 of the ICOM Model Rules (see Appendix B).

A substantial part of the profits should be ploughed back into the enterprise. This is absolutely necessary and will be crucial to the survival of a co-operative, especially in its early years. For reasons connected with the money market which are explained in any sound textbook on economics or business management, no business can expect to survive if it tries to obtain all its capital from outside sources. Unless it creates a substantial reserve from retained profits it will fail, and this is particularly so in the case of a co-operative, which initially is likely to have few assets which it can offer as security for loans and which is also likely to have an unattractive image for outside sources of finance, both because of its unorthodox control structure and because of its probable denial to outside investors of the chance of participation in profits.

It is therefore imperative that a substantial part of any profits be allocated to a general reserve fund; apart from the need for such a fund to provide for such things as re-equipment and expansion, it is highly likely to be needed to see the co-operative through difficult trading conditions and the unforeseen happenings which afflict every commercial enterprise.

It is sometimes argued that the members of a co-operative cannot be trusted to vote sufficient to reserve because the more they put to reserve the less there will be to distribute amongst themselves, but there is no reason why the members of a co-operative should be any less prudent in this respect than the shareholders of a 'traditional' company. If the ordinary shareholders vote themselves too large a dividend at the expense of the reserves, the company will become inefficient and the shareholders may lose their money, or at least the value of their shares will go down. If the members of a co-operative vote themselves too much they are likely to lose their jobs, and if the co-operative fails they are also likely to lose any money they may have lent to it.

Some of the profits can be used for charitable, social or community purposes. The motivation of those who start co-operatives is often at least partly charitable or social. It is therefore natural that they should favour the use of part of any profits for such purposes, and apart from any question of the founders' motivation it is found in practice that when the going gets rough a commitment to some purpose other than the material benefit of the members, particularly to the local community, can help to hold the enterprise together. Other causes which have benefited from the profits of existing workers' co-operatives are the Third World, the disabled and handicapped, and other enterprises which are starting, or converting to, a co-operative structure.

Having allocated a prudent amount of the profits to general reserve, and possibly an amount to charity, the members can then distribute what is left to themselves, and two questions arise. Should it be in cash, and on what basis should they share it?

The ICOM Model Rules mention 'as a bonus', but this does not necessarily mean 'in cash', and bearing in mind the desirability of as much financing of the enterprse as possible from retained profits, we suggest that consideration should be given to the Mondragon capital credits system described in Case Study 5. This allows the enterprise to have the use of distributed profits though each member 'has his name' on part of them. The withdrawal conditions need not necessarily be as arduous as those imposed at Mondragon.

The question of how profits should be shared out can be looked at in two ways. Some co-operators argue that, if everyone is pulling his weight, effort is equal and distribution should be equal. Others feel that hours worked, skill and responsibility are all a measure of contribution to the profits and should therefore be taken into account in any distribution. In this case distribution in proportion to wages earned might be considered fair, but this is really a matter for the members to decide amongst themselves.

There is one point which, though not directly connected with the distribution of profits, does have a bearing on the self-financing of an enterprise and can conveniently be discussed here.This is the question of entrance fees for membership. Some co-operatives think these are essential to provide a sense of commitment, others do not, and again this is a question for the members to decide. Such fees do provide capital, but it is difficult to imagine the £1,000 required at Mondragon, which itself only amounts to 5% of the capital required to provide one job, being acceptable in Britain. One of the ICOM companies requires a commitment on joining of six months' earnings which is deductible from wages over a period of four years.

As a conclusion to this section we shall return to the theme of retained profits. Restraint by the members in distributing cash to themselves, particularly in the early years, will 'pay dividends' later in the form of more money for distribution. In fact it may well be the factor which determines whether the co-operative survives or fails.

11. How can associations of co-operatives be formed ?

Many of the more recently formed co-operatives have shown interest in various forms of associations between co-operatives. These developments attempt to form different structures which combine the collective assets of individual firms, share services and resources, provide a sheltered start-up environment, or ensure a closer involvement from the local community.

Many of these developments are still at the experimental stage and hence what follows is no more than a brief outline to indicate what might be possible and what might be worth consideration. We have found it helpful to divide the types of association into five categories and to give each a 'short-hand' title:

  i) Initiating and holding companies - 'top-down promotion'
 ii) Co-operatives of co-operatives - 'bottom-up growth'

iii) Commonwealths - 'sideways development'
iv) Trade associations - 'informal links'
v) Community companies - 'geographical base'

We give a brief description of the main characteristics of each category and then go on to discuss legal structures and give some examples.

i) Initiating and holding companies: top-down promotion

This type of association has characteristics similar to the group system often employed by big business. A holding company is set up whose function is to administer, and in the last resort to control, a number of subsidiaries (the individual co-operatives forming the group). The holding company takes entrepreneurial initiatives and provides central services (legal, financial, accountancy, technical, marketing etc.). Obviously this system is open to criticism on the grounds of paternalism and absence of co-operative 'purity', but such considerations must be weighed against the difficulties likely to be experienced by small groups of would-be co-operators trying to go it alone in breaking into a harsh commercial environment, (see also Section 5 'the Pre Co-op System'). This structure can be especially relevant for groups of people who wish to encourage and assist the formation of co-operatives in their area. Individual enterprises initiated by the parent company might eventually become fully independent co-operatives.

ii) Co-operatives of co-operatives: bottom-up growth

In this type of association a number of established co-operatives voluntarily group together to provide themselves with certain facilities or services or to strengthen their financial or marketing muscle. Each wishes, however, to retain its own autonomy, so they form a joint co-operative which is owned and controlled by its member co-operatives. Control here is from the bottom upwards, the opposite to i) above.

iii)Commonwealths: sideways development

This type of association occurs when a co-operative grows and finds that it has become involved in a number of disparate operations and it becomes evident that although there is still a need for a centralised legal structure to provide administrative services and general co-ordination, each operation could have a separate trading name and be responsible for its own production, and possibly also marketing, functions. The co-operative therefore splits itself into a number of units which, although self-managed locally, are nevertheless tied to one another by a legal structure. The workers' ownership is of the whole co-operative and not just of the self-managed local unit in which they work.

iv) Trade Associations: informal links

A number of co-operatives which are in a similar line of business but do not wish to tie themselves to one another in any formal, legal way may establish a Trade Association with the object of promoting or protecting their common interests or arranging distributive networks. Many such Associations exist in the conventional business world with the purpose of agreeing price structures, conducting negotiations with various authorities and agreeing a common policy towards impending legislation, etc.

v) Community companies: geographical base

In some areas of the country the local community, in the form of community groups, local councillors and officials, local businessmen, Trades Councils, the churches and young people who want to stay and work in the area, has begun to try collectively to create new enterprises. The object is to create home-grown jobs which depend on local initiative and skills rather than on outside support.

This type of initiative has led to the formation of community companies which are trading organisations based on co-operative membership of the residents from a geographical area. The workers in the various enterprises of a community company are employees of the community company and are not worker owners. A significant proportion of the profits of such a company will be returned to community benefit and starting capital can sometimes be raised for this type of association through contributions from the residents of the area of benefit.

Legal structures

Those contemplating the formation of some sort of association should first decide exactly what it is that they wish to create and then examine what legal structure will be most appropriate. The only source of examples and experience so far is to consult those who have already created one form of association or another. Three points in particular should be considered.

First, the legal structure of an association generally needs to be tailor made to fit the objectives and working methods of its members and much time and thought will be needed to ensure that it does.

Second, it is well established that co-operation between individuals, even in a small co-operative, is by no means automatic; how much more difficult may it be to achieve in a collection of co-operatives?

Third, how much will the evils of 'bigness' be allowed to creep in, and how much autonomy will individual co-operatives have to surrender to the association if it is to serve any useful purpose?

In those categories where a legal structure is required (i, ii, iii, and v above) it is possible to use either company law or co-operative law. In general company law allows rather more flexibility than co-operative law and future constitutional changes are therefore more readily made. It is unlikely that there will be any significant difference in cost whether registration is as a company or as a co-operative. What is essential is for the group to know what structure it wants **before** taking legal action and to ensure that the structure adopted reflects properly the desired relationship between the association and its members.

An initiating or holding company (category i) could be constituted either as a Registered Co-operative or as a Company and the same is true for a co-operative of co-operatives (category ii). For reasons of flexibility a Company Limited by Guarantee is probably more suitable for an initiating or holding company while a Registered Co-operative would be more in keeping for the growth of a co-operative of co-operatives.

In the case of a commonwealth (category iii) it is probable that the existing legal structure of the original co-operative would continue unchanged, because sideways development is concerned more with the internal organisation of a growing enterprise than with changes in ownership or legal structure.

A community company (category v) can be structured either as a Registered Co-operative or as a Company, both having been successfully used in different parts of the country.

Some examples

We hope that our tentative establishment of five specific categories of association may help to clarify the thinking of those interested in this aspect of co-operative development, but it has to be said that many existing associations possess characteristics which belong to more than one category. For this reason none of the examples which follow has been allocated to any particular category.

One of the best known and most successful examples of an association of co-operatives is the Mondragon organisation in the Basque region of Spain and this is described in Case Study 5. In Britain there is as yet nothing so far advanced.

Alternative Co-operative Enterprises (A.C.E.) of Milton Keynes is a co-operative which acts as an umbrella company for new enterprises set up by its members. Initially new enterprises are established as subsidiaries of A.C.E. but the intention is that they eventually become independent workers' co-operatives.

A number of loose trade associations have been established between British worker co-operatives working in wholefoods, book selling and printing. Collaboration ranges from the simple exchange of information to the development of collective production, import, wholesale and distribution networks.

In the Northampton area a co-operative which is involved in a number of different trading operations has recently re-organised itself as Northampton Industrial Commonwealth (N.I.C.). There are central financial, administrative and organisational services but the different units of operation have a degree of self-management and are responsible for organising their own work. N.I.C. is an ICOM Model Rules co-operative.

In Newry and Mourne, Northern Ireland, a recently formed co-operative society acts both as a property company providing factory space and as a holding company with three subsidiaries, a development company, an enterprise making play equipment and a craft workshop. Much of the finance for this initiative was raised by the sale of shares to members of the local community.

In Scotland the Highlands and Islands Development Board (H.I.D.B.) launched in 1977 a Community Co-operative Scheme aimed at encouraging economically depressed (and mainly island) communities to form multi-functional trading organisations owned and controlled by local residents. Members contribute share capital which is matched £ for £ by the H.I.D.B. but the co-operative structure ensures a system of one member, one vote.

In the Craigmillar district of Edinburgh the local Community Association has created its own trading company, Craigmillar Festival Enterprises Ltd, (C.F.E.L.), whose object is to create jobs for local people. C.F.E.L. is a Company Limited by Guarantee owned and controlled by the local residents through the Executive Committee of their Community Association. Any profits made will return to the local community and will not benefit individual members of the company, and consequently C.F.E.L. has been granted charitable status.

Summary

We emphasise the importance of working out clearly what is wanted before embarking on any legal steps and we stress the importance of finding out first-hand what others have done. Most groups with some experience of associations can be contacted through the organisations listed in Section A of Appendix A.

12. Epilogue

We have called Part II 'The Mechanics of Workers' Co-operatives'.

The word 'mechanics' comes from a Greek word meaning 'how to make something work', and it is in this light that we intend Part II to be read. For instance, traditional practice and attitudes may have to be modified, and we have suggested where the difficulties in doing this may lie; some legal and financial structures may be more appropriate than others, and we have tried to explain why; but no amount of mechanics will create a workers' co-operative if the basic principles are not recognised, agreed and observed.

What these principles should be has been debated in co-operative circles since they days of the Rochdale Pioneers, but we would state them again as:

1. Full control by the workforce, both 'management' and 'workers'.
2. 'One man, one vote'.
3. Labour hires capital, not vice versa.
4. No dissolution for personal gain.

There may be a case in the early stages of an enterprise for some modification of Principle 1 and, by implication, of Principle 2, but unless all four principles are agreed at the start as the ultimate aim and unless everyone works towards their achievement, the result is likely to be an unsatisfactory compromise and will not, in our opinion, be a genuine **workers'** co-operative.

III. THE FUTURE OF WORKER CO-OPERATION IN BRITAIN

This handbook has been written for intending members of workers' co-operatives as a practical guide to the key questions which must be faced in setting up a co-operative enterprise. Individual co-operatives are, however, part of a growing worker co-operative movement and of the wider economic structure. The future for all co-operators will therefore depend not only on the economic viability of their particular co-operative but also on the political, social and economic climate within which co-operatives have to exist and develop regionally, nationally and internationally. In this final part of the handbook we look briefly at some of the factors that could influence and determine that climate.

High unemployment and new enterprises

It has been said that 'we are on the edge of a sombre decade'. As the economic situation has worsened and unemployment risen there has been growing dissatisfaction at the failure of existing regional and economic policies to counter the loss of jobs and alleviate urban deprivation and, at the same time, a growing interest in ways of creating new jobs in new enterprises at the local level. Political parties and Government, Local Authorities and the business community have all turned their attention to ways in which the small business sector can be encouraged to grow.

As we have suggested in Part I of this handbook the worsening economic situation has been accompanied by an unprecedented growth in almost every sector of worker co-operative development as an increasing number of people seek not only to create their own jobs but to control and organise them in a more democratic and humane way. More than 300 co-operatives are now registered in the United Kingdom; there has been legislation in the form of the Industrial Common Ownership, Inner Urban Areas and Co-operative Development Agency Acts; a number of local and national co-operative development bodies have been created, and many local and national public bodies now recognise that the encouragement of co-operatives should form part of their work. Evidently there is a growing interest in the part that the co-operative sector might play in the development of employment opportunities.

The need for political commitment

The workers' co-operative movement is part of a reaction against bigness and represents a trend towards decentralisation and smaller, more understandable units of working. It is part of a growing third sector in the economy which rejects the bureaucracy of public ownership and the profit-centred ruthlessness of big business and private enterprise and the endless confrontation between capital and labour. If, however, co-operation is to become more than a fringe activity of idealists it has both to prove its case economically and to foster a political commitment to this third way.

Co-operators, by their nature and beliefs, tend to prefer working at the local level, demonstrating the success and viability of their own enterprises in the local economy. Many of the new co-operatives operate in the service sector of industry with low overheads and small capital requirements. The main concern of most workers in co-operatives is with the internal working of their individual enterprise so that they get what they need from their work both in terms of wages and in terms of the way the work is organised.

Despite the vicissitudes of recent years, a growing number of co-operatives have slowly been establishing themselves as valuable parts of local economies throughout the United Kingdom and their survival rate overall compares well with the failure rate of small business generally. It will be important, however, that local commercial success is matched by a growth of understanding and commitment at national level and there are a number of positive steps which government could take to encourage the growth of the co-operative sector. Corporation Tax payable by co-operatives could be reduced, perhaps to the same rate as that paid by individuals (30%). The liability to Capital Gains Tax or Capital Transfer Tax could be abolished for shareholders in companies which convert to co-operatives, the assets being turned into indivisible reserves. A preferential rate of Value Added Tax could be introduced for co-operatives as has been done in Spain. Special loan guarantee schemes and other forms of financial assistance could be provided especially for co-operatives.

Such developments will only come about if politicians actually wish there to be a strong co-operative sector in the economy and make a commitment to seeing the necessary steps taken in the face of probable hostility from private enterprise and scepticism from the Trades Unions. It is to be hoped that the all party support for the Co-operative Development Agency Bill heralds the beginning of that political commitment. Likewise it has been encouraging in recent months to hear politicians of all parties thinking aloud about the common sense and innate fairness of co-operation, blending as it does collective ownership and community responsibility with individual initiative and entrepreneurial flair.

One part of the political arena which could significantly stimulate the growth of the workers' co-operative movement is the Trade Unions. They hold the means of influencing the thinking of working people and they could promote educational and information programmes to aid understanding of co-operation. In addition they control substantial funds which could well be applied to the creation of worker controlled enterprises and they have a strength of bargaining power which could greatly reinforce negotiations with industry, Government and local financial institutions. Regrettably Trade Union interest in worker ownership and co-operation has until now fallen short of wholehearted and enthusiastic support, while the absence of union affiliation in some co-operatives has not helped matters.

Community support

One of the strengths of the worker co-operative movement is that it has in most cases been a growth from the 'bottom-up'. People get together to form their own enterprise because they want to own it collectively and to run it democratically. Members of workers' co-operatives and other interested people form local Co-operative Development Groups to encourage the formation of new co-operatives in their area. Such grass-roots growth usually has close links with the local community and with those other manifestations of the co-operative spirit: credit unions and community enterprises. It is not coincidental that many co-operatives include in their constitutions a clause about benefiting the local community in some way.

Support for co-operatives often comes in particular from those areas most affected by cuts in state spending and by rising unemployment. The desire to create businesses which involve the community with its own economic development rather than leaving things to the whims of multi-national finance has brought together new alliances of Trades Councils, Chambers of Commerce, Local Authorities, voluntary groups and unemployed people in an attempt to fight local decline. Community involvement and support has led to experimentation with new legal and financial structures which can raise and channel local financial support and provide technical and other advice. In some cases these develop into groups servicing and supporting autonomous co-operative enterprises; in others they initiate enterprises which may later become autonomous co-operatives.

Mutual support and the wider economy

Co-operatives need to survive in the harsh reality of the market economy and for individual co-operatives that can be a lonely battle which has led to the growth of mutual help. New co-operatives have found that much of the best advice and assistance can come from older established ones and in some areas trade associations or federations have been formed to combine resources, to share problems and to offer practical and economic assistance to one another. In Italy the recent development of 'holding-companies' for co-operatives is a further extension of this idea. Although each individual co-operative retains its practical autonomy, the holding company organises within a particular industrial sector the distribution of raw materials to individual co-operatives, the sale of goods, the raising of finance and the negotiation of contracts, and provides advice. A further development to explore will be how far associations or federations can generate new capital collectively from their own member firms, either to sponsor new enterprises or to finance growth.

In Italy and France, Poland and Yugoslavia, large industrial co-operatives play a significant role in the economy, in contrast to Britain where the co-operative sector is small and predominantly in service industry. Although there is a strong wish to see more manufacturing co-operatives formed it is not at all clear how that can be achieved. Large amounts of investment would be required and in the current state of the economy it is hard both to see from where such capital might come and to identify the product areas in which it should be invested. A central dilemma for the co-operative movement during the eighties will be how to survive while at the same time developing away from the service and sub-contract sectors which so often rise and fall according to the plans of multi-national and large national corporations.

Education and promotion

Co-operation is an ideal which has not been a natural part of British attitudes and values for many generations; it goes against the competitive and individual ethos which has underpinned the character and thinking of the western capitalist nations at least since the industrial revolution. No co-operative will succeed unless the members want to co-operate, and the desire to co-operate will only be present where people understand the ideal, see it as relevant to them and are committed to turning it into a reality. To achieve that measure of understanding in our present day society is a difficult educational challenge. The teaching of co-operation must therefore be an important element in the future work of the movement and successful co-operatives must be well publicised so that people begin to see them not only as an ideal but also as a viable means of providing an adequate livelihood.

People who are interested in setting up co-operatives are often hampered by a lack of hard skills and they must be given the opportunity to obtain management, marketing and technical expertise for work situations which differ substantially from conventional business. Those brought up in large scale industrial situations where there is no apparent limit to resources cannot readily adjust to the small scale undercapitalised business environment, and conventional management courses, apart from being expensive, are often out of touch with the realities of co-operative life. There is thus a need to develop training courses and to modify existing consultancy and advisory services to cater specifically for the needs of co-operative and other small business management. Proposals have in fact been made to establish 'technical resource teams' which can help new co-operatives and provide support until they are well established.

Into the 1980s

The problems facing potential and existing workers' co-operatives should not be underestimated. They will be no more exempt than anyone else from the economic exigencies of the next few years. Indeed as small businesses and as a movement serving the needs and aspirations of people mostly without capital resources, workers' co-operatives are amongst the most vulnerable, particularly in a time of recession. The internal dynamics of any co-operative enterprise are not easy to live with and at the same time the co-operative must compete successfully in a ruthless market place.

The dice are not, however, by any means loaded all one way. It is becoming evident that full employment, in the sense that everyone can work maximum hours for maximum pay, will not be attainable in Britain in the future, and there will have to be a re-thinking of the way work is allocated. Either fewer people can work long hours at high hourly rates or the available work can be shared out amongst more people working less hours for an adequate but lower total wage.

No sudden changes in the way industry operates are going to occur and any change that does come about will probably be accompanied by resistance, but to many people, particularly perhaps younger people, the second system outlined above seems preferable, and workers' co-operatives, offering as they do an absence of bosses and a concern for values other than maximum material gain, are in a strong position to demonstrate how that second system can be at least partially achieved.

Most of the co-operatives set up since the publication of the Scottish Handbook in 1977 are now emerging as stable and healthy enterprises. The new co-operative movement is flourishing with a small but strong base and there are thus indications that workers' co-operatives could have an increasing part to play in the industrial development of our country. Their future role will depend on the existing co-operatives being able to demonstrate that it is possible to work to the co-operative ideal and earn an adequate wage at the same time. It will also depend on politicians committing themselves to the co-operative ideal and being prepared to enact legislation which will encourage the growth of co-operative enterprises. It will depend on a changing of attitudes as people come to place more emphasis on democracy at work, on a pleasant working atmosphere, on quality rather than on quantity.

Our hope is that democracy in the workplace will become as much a part of the fabric of our society as political democracy.

CASE STUDIES

1. A plant hire and building co-operative

Mr. X came out of the Army in 1948 and by the early 1970's had built up a thriving contractors' hire business with 25 lorries, 60 machines (principally hydraulic excavators) with operators, a variety of other machines and a total workforce of 120. The business was then sold to company Y operating in the same field and Mr. X joined company Y on a service contract. Subsequently this was regretted because of the unsatisfactory and impersonal relationships between management and employees in company Y and Mr. X because interested in starting a new business venture along workers' co-operative common ownership lines.

Because of the possible legal problems regarding his service contract he could take no formal position in any new venture, but he was able to ensure that capital together with business experience was available to assist his two nephews (one a qualified engineer and the other a skilled plant fitter), and an experienced plant operator, to establish a plant hire company Z, a Company Limited by Shares. In 1976 company Z was converted to a co-operative registered under the I & PS Acts, using Section 53 of the 1965 Act and the ICOM Model Rules, and by the end of that year it had a total workforce of 16 and 13 machines.

Overall policy, wage rates and admittance to Membership are decided by a General Meeting which meets every four weeks and consists of all the Members of the Co-operative.
Originally all employees, no matter how short their length of service, were entitled to attend and vote at the General Meeting, but this arrangement was not found to give stable, far-sighted management of the company's affairs and has now

been modified. Under the new arrangements a new employee does not attend the General Meetings during the first three months of his employment, then is entitled to attend them, but not to vote, for the next six months. At the end of his nine month probationary period he can apply to be elected a Member of the co-operative by the vote of the General Meeing, and this system, which is in accordance with Rule 6(b) of the ICOM Model Rules and Section 2(1)(b) of the ICO Act, seems to work to everyone's satisfaction.

Day to day decisions, such as the movement of machines and operators from job to job, are taken by the manager and his immediate staff. Other business decisions are taken by the management committee of seven which is elected by the Members in General Meeting, meets every week, and currently includes the three original directors; another elected committee decides what plant to buy and what employees should be taken on.

Members are encouraged to lend money to the co-operative, and receive interest at Minimum Lending Rate + 1%, but there is no share system other than the £1 'membership ticket' required by the Model Rules. Most members do make loans, on the basis that they make available what they can afford.

Mr. X now has no obligations to company Y and has been unanimously elected a member of the co-operative. Long term finance has been found from other sources and he sees his role as being on hand to train and educate the members into being able to take a full share in the responsibilities of operating a viable commercial common ownership enterprise.

This example shows what can be accomplished by a combination of trust, common sense and a determination at all levels to 'make it work'. It combines commercial efficiency with worker control and ownership, and all these objectives seem to have been achieved.

2. Recycles

Recycles opened in Edinburgh in 1977 as a bicycle repair shop in the old part of the city. It was started by three friends, all unemployed, all with an interest in bikes, who decided that the only way they would get jobs would be by making their own. As cyclists they knew there was a need for a repair shop and repairing bikes was something they knew about. The idea was spurred into action when they found a small inexpensive shop. Initial finance came from friends, relations and from the bank on security of their flat.

Recycles did repairs and sold second-hand bikes. The shop was small. Wages were the maximum which avoided income tax and national insurance (£14.99 at that time). Although there was work it was not enough to pay all three an adequate wage. Nor did they have enough space for additional activities.

After six months one of the three returned to the dole queue while he explored setting up a cycle hire operation. They were certain there was a market and at the same time an academic exercise carried out at Edinburgh University Business Studies School confirmed the apparent viability of the idea and strengthened their case for funds.

Suitable premises were found and with a small loan from Industrial Common Ownership Finance and further loans from friends, Edinburgh Cycle Hire got underway just in time for summer 1978. Hiring bikes has led in turn to a growing retail and spares trade and increased repair work. By summer 1979 the co-operative had increased to six working members and two temporary staff, and wages were raised to £50 per week.

Recycles started as a co-operative because 'we wanted to organise a business so that it was controlled by the workers'. Decisions are made at a weekly meeting and although rotation of jobs is aimed at, each worker is responsible for different tasks for periods long enough to be consistent with efficiency. Financial control is recognised as vital but is sometimes neglected: 'it is particularly important in a small business, where no one has complete authority, where no one has the full-time job of doing it. It tends to fall between other things and gets picked up more often than not as a crisis arises'.

The workers at Recycles emphasise the importance of trust between workers, of instilling confidence in financial backers whether they are friends or the Bank, and the responsibilities which the pleasure of working for yourself can bring: 'You have to be determined, you have to want to work with others on an equal basis. You have to see some fruit from that labour, you have to see that it is going to be pleasurable for you. The difficulty is that you have the responsibility as well as the pleasure of it'.

3. Calverts North Star Press

Calverts North Star Press Limited has been trading as a common ownership co-operative since November 1977. Its birth in this form stemmed from a decision by a group of workers who were the printing division of a small theatrical publishing group, which in theory was a co-operative but whose true legal and ownership structure was revealed when the owner of the £100 share company threatened half the work-force with the sack.

After four months of struggle with the owner of the company, trying to persuade him to turn it into a proper common ownership co-operative, seven print workers handed in 'constructive resignations' and started putting their efforts into forming a new co-operative press. We had learnt our first lesson - don't rely on trust in your working situation; make sure that your legal and ownership status is clear and unambiguous right from the start.

Initially we applied for an MSC grant by producing a feasability study with financial, technical, marketing, and organisational information. We were, however, refused for two reasons, one reasonable - that we were not intending to employ enough old or young people, and one ridiculous - that we were not going to provide a service that other printers in London were not providing already. In retrospect, however, we are glad that we did not get a grant to pay our wages, because it meant we had to survive by our own efforts. We realised that we were a 'business' which had commitments to its employees in terms of conditions and security of employment, wages etc., and also to its customers in terms of speed, quality, etc. We managed, though, to get a loan of £6,000 through ICOF (Industrial Common Ownership Finance Limited) which meant that we could invest in new plant allowing us to do better quality, better paid work. Our present turnover is around £7,200 a month with 9 workers.

Calvert's is registered under ICOM Model Rules, which allow for no outside shareholders (and thus no outside control) and members' (workers') share capital can only be a nominal £1 each. Capital can be raised by means of loans which are registered as debenture loan stock.

We have added to these ICOM rules various other regulations and principles that we feel are important to the running of a co-operative.

1. That a monthly meeting of **all** members shall act as the management of the co-operative and be responsible for making policy decisions, ratifying appointments, approving membership of the co-operative and determining the financial priorities.
2. That a weekly meeting makes production decisions i.e. planning work for the coming week, employing people etc.
3. That we do not operate a system of job rotation like some co-operatives as we see this as incompatible with the necessity for developing skills (printing is a five years appren-

ticeship). However, we do operate a system of job transfer where members may apply to the general meeting to do a different task (giving 3 months notice).
4. That the co-operative is a common ownership company established for the purpose of advancing the cause of collective ownership of the means of production under workers' control.

At present we are earning £70 for a 35 hour week or £85 for 42 hours, but are aiming for the average industrial wage in the short term. All workers earn equal wages. Some of our potential earnings (maybe £15 a week each) goes towards subsidies on jobs whose publishers have no printing budgets e.g. community groups, campaigning organisations, etc.

Two important aspects of our survival have been external and internal support. First we have been helped enormously by a solid body of customers and friends who have appreciated what we are trying to do and prefer to give their material to a co-operative. In return we operate three price scales depending on the type and the financial position of the customer. Secondly, as a result of our fight at our previous firm there has been a great feeling of solidarity amongst the members of the co-op, resulting in a strong determination to make a genuine co-operative succeed. We have progressed from being on the dole, through earning pitiful wages to a situation where we now work normal hours for acceptable money in the sort of workplace we can enjoy. There is no denying it has been hard work on the way, but well worth it.

4. Triangle Wholefoods Collective (Suma)

Triangle Wholefoods trades as Suma, a wholefood wholesaling outlet, started in 1975 with approximately £4,000 capital which was gradually introduced throughout the first year of trading. For the first two years it was officially a sole ownership enterprise but it was in fact run collectively from the start.

For the first year it was run half time by two people, one of whom had another full-time job, with help from friends. They used a tiny storage space and by their efforts were able to build up capital and towards the end of the first year two other workers joined and the business started to operate as a co-operative.

Suma's original customers (retail shops) formed the Federation of Northern Wholefood Collectives (FNWC) and this has now largely devolved itself into smaller regional groupings. To be a member of the FNWC it is necessary to be a registered co-operative and to be committed to improving food quality. Suma has been an important focal point for the FNWC, helping the formation of new co-operatives as it had itself been helped by the support of the retail shops in the first place.

Suma has now grown to become a substantial business employing 12 people at a living wage and with a turnover in excess of £1m each year. There are some specific job functions, although these are flexible and can be rotated, and as the business has grown, workers have tended to stay with one group of tasks longer than was the case in the early years.

The business closes every Wednesday afternoon and an often lengthy meeting discusses matters of policy and exchanges grievances and complaints. All working conditions, including wages, are decided at these meetings. It is the aim of the collective that facilities should be much better than those in a conventional work-place.

In 1976 Suma set up a wholefood retail shop (Beano) in Leeds. This was supported by Suma in its early months, but became a completely independent co-operative in 1978. Suma itself became a registered co-operative in 1977. We would recommend any group considering working collectively to accept the legal responsibility of registering themselves as a co-operative.

It has been the experience of Suma members that co-

operative working tends to become a way of life, so that former
members have returned to Suma after spells in conventional
employment. Other ex-members have been instrumental in
the founding of other co-operatives, including a real ale
off-licence and a food processing factory.

5. The Mondragon organisation

Over the past twenty years an organisation has grown around
the small manufacturing town of Mondragon in the Basque
region of Northern Spain in which there are now seventy
workers' co-operatives with a total workforce of 15,000 and
an annual turnover of some £200 million. Each co-operative
is autonomous and run by a Control Board elected annually
but there is a central banking agency financed by the co-
operatives to provide financial, banking and advisory services.

'One man, one vote' applies throughout the organisation.
When a worker joins a capital account is opened in his name
and to this is credited 75% of the entrance fee (usually £1,000)
which he is either required to pay immediately or to have de-
ducted from his wages over a period of two years. The remaining 25% passes to the general reserves of the enterprise.
Each member is given a job rating on a points system from 1
to 3, the figure 2 on the scale representing the average wage
in 'traditional' industry outside the organisation. Wages for
normal working and overtime are paid monthly in cash on the
basis of the worker's job rating.

Profits are allocated annually; a minimum of 30% to general
reserve, 40% credited to members' accounts in proportion to
their job ratings and 10% to the local community. Fixed interest on the amount of each member's account is paid in cash
annually. If, however, an enterprise gets into difficulties

members are expected to help, by having payments for overtime and interest on their accounts credited to their accounts instead of being paid in cash. Members may withdraw the whole of their accumulated capital account on retirement and some have built up amounts of £10,000 - £15,000, exclusive of normal pension. Those who leave before retirement may, except in special circumstances, risk forfeiting up to 20% of their accounts. Accounts can be written up to compensate for inflation, but if the co-operative makes losses its members' accounts can also be written down.

Space does not permit further discussion of this system in this handbook, but it may be useful to point out some advantages. Commitment is encouraged by entrance fees and the building up of personal 'capital credits', which are at risk if the co-operative does not fare well financially but which also provide a means of individual saving and a fund against which a member can borrow whilst still working and which he can withdraw when he retires. Profits are allocated according to effort, not capital contributed, and there is a large element of self-financing by the organisation, which has the use not only of profits ploughed back into general reserve but also of profits retained in members' capital accounts. Finally, a continuing commitment to the local community, which is fundamental to the Mondragon concept, is ensured by the existence of a school and polytechnic established, owned and managed by the co-operatives which together make up the Mondragon organisation.

(Readers wishing further information should consult **Worker Owners - The Mondragon Achievement**: see Appendix G).

APPENDICES

APPENDIX A

Some important resources available to workers' co-operatives in Britain

A. Those specialising in assistance to co-operatives

Co-operative Development Agency, 20 Albert Embankment, London SE1 7TJ 01-211-7033

established by Government in 1978 to promote all forms of co-operation, to do research, education and information work and advise on legislation.

Industrial Common Ownership Movement Ltd., Beechwood College, Elmete Lane, Roundhay, Leeds L88 2LQ 0532-651235

membership organisation for individuals and co-operatives; sponsor of model rules for registration as a co-operative; general advice and assistance; has regional groups and a conference centre.

Co-operative Union Limited, Holyoake House, Hanover Street, Manchester M60 0AS 061-834-0975

national federation of the traditional co-operative movement.

Co-operative Productive Federation, 30 Wandsworth Bridge Road, London SW6 01-736-4514/01-499-5991

federation of the 'old' producer co-operatives of the traditional Co-operative movement.

Scottish Co-operatives Development Committee Limited, 100 Morrison Street, Glasgow 041-429-1488

information and advice to Workers' Co-operatives in Scotland.

Job Ownership Limited, 42/44 Hanway Street, London W1P 9DE 01-637-0780

advises, in particular, groups wishing to adopt a Mondragon style 'capital ownership' structure and companies wishing to convert to employee ownership.

Co-operatives Research Unit, Faculty of Technology, The Open University, Walton Hall, Milton Keynes, MK7 6AA 0908-63826

carries out research about co-operatives and co-operative practice; organises seminars and courses.

Commonwork Limited, Bore Place, Bough Beech, Edenbridge, Kent Weald 255

an educational trust specialising in work on worker management; arranges seminars and courses in association with the Co-operatives Research Unit; has a small residential conference centre.

Registrar of Friendly Societies, 17 North Audley Street, London W17 2AP 01-629-7001

assistance on registering as a workers' co-operative.

Assistant Registrar of Friendly Societies, 19 Heriot Row, Edinburgh 031-556-4371

Local Co-operative Development Groups:

In the last two years a number of local and regional advisory groups for workers' co-operatives have been set up. In some cases they are branches of ICOM, in others they are independent local groupings of various interests.

Lists of addresses can be obtained from ICOM, from the CDA and from the Co-operatives Research Unit. Addresses of Local Enterprise Trusts can be obtained from Intermediate Technology Development Group (see below).

B. Those which can provide financial and other assistance

Industrial Common Ownership Finance Ltd., 4 St. Giles Street, Northampton NN1 1AA 0604-37563	a loan fund exclusively for workers' co-operatives.
Co-operative Bank Limited, Head Office, P.O Box 101, New Century House, Manchester M4 8BE 061-834-8687	although it announced a loan scheme for workers' co-operatives, it will deal with applications exactly like any other bank and will look for substantial member contributions; start with your local co-operative bank manager.
Department of Employment	use the local job centre for initial information and make contact with regional offices throughout Britain.
Department of Industry, Small Firms Division, Abell House, John Islip Street, London SW1P 4LL 01-211-3000	there are regional offices throughout Britain; grants towards machinery, plant and buildings; loans and other assistance under the Industry Act 1972; counselling service.
Manpower Services Commission, Selkirk House, 166 High Holborn, London WC1V 6PF 01-836-1213	there are regional offices throughout Britain; limited funds exist for Enterprise Workshops which can be structured as co-operatives.
Council for Small Industries, in Rural Areas (Cosira), 11 Cowley Street, London SW1 01-222-9134	also regional offices in England; loans and grants; general advice and guidance; consultancy service.
Scottish Development Agency, Small Business Division, 102 Telford Road, Edinburgh EH4 2NP 031-343-1911	grants and loans; general advice and guidance; factories; rent free periods; consultancy service.

Welsh Development Agency,
Small Business Unit,
Treforest Industrial Estate,
Nr. Pontypridd,
Mid Glamorgan CF37 5UT
Treforest 2666

grants and loans; general advice
and guidance; factories; rent free
periods; consultancy service.

Highlands and Islands
Development Board,
Bridge House,
Bank Street,
Inverness IV1 1QR
0463-34171

information and advice in the
Highlands and Islands of Scotland, consultancy service, loans
and grants, and assistance to
community co-operatives.

Banks are the biggest lenders of money to small businesses. Start
with your local bank manager. Much will depend on what he thinks
about co-operatives and how well you can impress him with your
plans and the way you present them.

C. Those who give general advice and help

Local Authorities

Local councils at all levels - District, County and Region - have a
variety of ways of helping firms.
These can include helping to find
premises, making loans, rent free
periods, general knowledge about
the area. Some have set up special units to give advice and help
to small firms and a few make
a particular attempt to assist in
the growth of co-operatives in
their area. Start inquiring at the
Chief Executive's Office.

Small Firms Information
Centres

These have been set up in the different regions of the country
by the Department of Industry
to act as a 'signposting service'
directing small businesses to the
right agency or person to help
solve their particular problem.
They also publish a particularly
valuable series of information
booklets which are available free

of charge. Find your regional SFIC by looking in the telephone book or asking at your local information centre or at the local council offices. In some areas SFIC have set up volunteer counselling services for small businesses.

Action Resource Centre,
4 Cromwell Place,
London SW7 2JJ
01-584-0438

arranges resources from industry, including personnel secondments, to projects of community benefit or to create new jobs.

Scottish Action Resource
Centre,
54 Shandwick Place,
Edinburgh EH2 42T
031-226-3669

Intermediate Technology
Development Group,
Wilton Corner,
10 Grenfell Road,
Beaconsfield,
Berks.
049-46-3080

supports and encourages the creation of Local Enterprise Trusts to advise and assist small businesses.

Charities Aid Fund,
48 Pembury Road,
Tonbridge,
Kent.
0732-63232

publishes a directory of grant-making trusts (also available in most public libraries).

Institute for Workers' Control,
Bertrand Russell House,
Gamble Street,
Nottingham NG7 4ET
0602-708318

various publications and seminars; conferences about worker control and self management.

National Council of Social
Service,
26 Bedford Square,
London WC
01-636-4066

acts as a clearing house for employment initiatives in the voluntary sector, arranges conferences and workshops and can provide contacts with local councils for voluntary service which can sometimes provide advice for groups interested in setting up co-operatives.

Scottish Council of Social
Service,
18/19 Claremont Crescent,
Edinburgh EH7 4QD
031-556-3882

In addition the following local agencies or organisations can provide useful information and help.

Employment Services Department Training Services Department Department of Employment	training opportunities, training grants, temporary unemployment subsidies, local manpower availability.
Department of Health and Social Security	about national insurance.
Inland Revenue	about the PAYE system and also about national insurance.
Customs and Excise	about Value Added Tax.
Industrial Training Boards	for advice and technical expertise
Trade Unions	for general advice and for goodwill and support.
Local Colleges	for technical expertise, for other specialist help (e.g. legal matters, accountancy etc.) and for help with feasability studies.
Chambers of Commerce	for contact with other business people and general business assistance.
Trade Associations	for contact with others in the same line of business.

Procedure for Registration as a Co-operative under the Industrial and Provident Societies Acts using the ICOM Model Rules, with copy of the rules

The Industrial Common Ownership Movement (ICOM) has prepared a set of Model Rules ('ICOM 1977') which can be registered under the Industrial and Provident Societies (I&PS)Acts and are acceptable for a certificate under the Industrial Common Ownership (ICO) Act 1976 (see Appendix D).

Under the I&PS Acts registration with model rules must be through a promoting body recognised by the Registrar of Friendly Societies and ICOM is such a body. Some groups may wish to consult a solicitor before making a final decision on their best method of registration and they may find it helpful first to consult their local Co-operative Development Group (see Appendix A for means for making contact) on the appropriateness of the I&PS Acts for the registration of their co-operative.

The group wishing to start the co-operative meet as the Founding Members. For registration under the I&PS Acts there must be at least seven of them and it is not necessary that all of them should be working in the co-operative (but see Rule 6(b) which accommodates the ICO Act and see also Appendix D). They proceed as follows:

1. They decide on a name for the enterprise. There is no legal requirement to use the word 'co-operative' in the name. The Registrar may reject names which are too similar to existing organisations, but under Section 53 of the I&PS Acts an existing limited company can change to a registered co-operative, and need not change its name in order to do so; i.e. PQR Ltd.,an incorporated company, can become PQR Ltd., a registered co-operative.

2. They write a preamble which outlines briefly the objectives of the co-operative, both commercial and social,

    and states that the enterprise is to be controlled by the people working in it. Examples of preambles can be obtained from local Co-operative Development Groups or from ICOM.

3. They appoint a Secretary who writes to ICOM sending the Preamble and a £20 annual subscription as an Associate Member of ICOM, and requesting the ICOM wallet called 'How to form an industrial co-operative' which contains copies of the Model Rules with explanatory notes and a complete set of the necessary forms and information needed for registration.

3a. Alternatively some groups may wish to receive advice from their local Co-operative Development Group before embarking on steps 1-3. They can obtain the wallet 'How to form an industrial co-operative' without committing themselves to Associate Membership of ICOM simply by sending £5 to ICOM.

4. The Founder Members and Secretary complete and sign 3 copies of the Rules and one copy of Form A, and return all these to ICOM with a cheque for £42 for the Registration Fee, made payable to the Registrar of Friendly Societies. All three copies of the Model Rules must be on the blank printed forms supplied by ICOM; the Registrar will not accept photo-copies. ICOM countersigns Form A as the sponsoring body and forwards it with the Model Rules and the cheque to the Registrar.

5. The Registrar returns one copy of the Rules to which is fixed the Registration Certificate giving the Number and Registration date. The co-operative is then a corporate body for trading purposes and has limited liability.

The Founder Members may add to or change the Model Rules if they wish but any proposed addition or alteration should first be discussed with ICOM and then negotiated directly with the Registrar. This may take considerably longer and the Registrar may charge the higher fee of £90 instead of £42 for the Model Rules unaltered. (However, minor changes may be acceptable both to ICOM and to the Registrar, who may still treat the rules as Model Rules and charge the reduced fee.)

Once a group starts to work together, the working members will need to agree on procedures for the day to day management of the enterprise. The internal procedures do not have the legal force of Registered Rules, and they may be changed from time to time by agreement among the Members. The Registered Rules can only be changed with the formal agreement of the Registrar.

Notes:

1. The ICOM Model Rules are reprinted by permission of the Industrial Common Ownership Movement. *They should not be reproduced and will not be accepted by the Registrar as model rules except through ICOM.*
2. We wish to thank ICOM for their assistance in compiling this appendix.
3. All fees and subscriptions were correct at 1.1.79 but are subject to annual revision.

COPY OF THE ICOM MODEL RULES (ICOM 1977)

RULES OF ....**LIMITED**
(registered under the Industrial and Provident Societies Acts 1965 -1975)

1. The NAME of the Society shall be ....
....
............Limited (hereinafter referred to as the Co-operative)

2. The OBJECTS of the Co-operative shall be to carry on the business as a bona fide co-operative society of
(a) Manufacturing or selling...
....
....
....
....
....
....

Providing the service of ....
....
....
....

(b) Manufacturing or selling or hiring whether as wholesalers, retailers, agents, or otherwise, such other goods (or providing such service) as may be determined by a General Meeting.

In carrying out the aforesaid objects the Co-operative shall have regard to promoting the physical, mental and spiritual well-being of the community and especially those who participate in the activities of the Co-operative by reason of employment in or purchasing from or selling to the Co-operative and to assist people in need by any means whatsoever.

3. POWERS. The Co-operative shall have power to do all things necessary or expedient for the fulfilment of its objects, provided that the assets of the Co-operative shall be applied only for the purposes of those objects which do not include the making over of assets to any member except for value and except in pursuance of arrangements for sharing the profits of the Co-operative among the members as provided for in Rule 14(b).

4. The REGISTERED OFFICE of the Co-operative shall be at
....
....

5. The SHARE CAPITAL of the Co-operative shall consist of shares of the nominal value of one pound each issued to persons upon admission to Membership of the Co-operative. The shares shall be neither withdrawable nor transferable, shall carry no right to interest dividend nor bonus and shall be forfeited and cancelled on cessation of membership from whatever cause and the amount paid-up thereon shall become the property of the Co-operative. A Member shall hold one share only in the Co-operative.

6. MEMBERSHIP
    (a) The Membership of the Co-operative shall consist of all those who sign the Application for Registration

(the Founder Members) and other persons. If an application is sent to the Chief Registrar of Friendly Societies for a certificate that the Co-operative is a common ownership enterprise, any Founder Member who is not employed by (or by a subsidiary of) the Co-operative on the date when the application is so sent shall cease to be a Member on that date provided that if the Registrar refuses to give such a certificate each such former Founder Member may elect to be readmitted as a Founder Member. Except for Founder Members (who shall be subject to the aforementioned provision as to cessation of their membership) only persons who are employed by (or by a subsidiary of) the Co-operative may be Members of it.

(b) All persons who are employed by (or by a subsidiary of) the Co-operative may be members, subject to any provision in the rules about qualifications for membership which is from time to time made by the Members, by reference to age, length of service, or other factors of any description which do not discriminate between persons by reference to politics or religion.

7. APPLICATION FOR MEMBERSHIP. On application for membership and the payment of £1 by any person qualifying under rule 6(b) above and who has attained the age of 18 years the Co-operative shall issue him or her with one share.

8. CESSATION OF MEMBERSHIP. A Member shall cease to be a Member if he or she:
(a) ceases to be in the employment of the Co-operative for any reason whatsoever.
(b) ceases to fulfil any other qualifications for membership specified in these rules.
(c) resigns in writing to the Secretary.
(d) dies.

9. BORROWING
(a) The Co-operative shall have power to borrow money for the purpose of the Co-operative in whatsoever manner it may determine including the issue of loan stock provided that the amount for the time being remaining undischarged of money borrowed shall not exceed £100,000.

(b) The rate of interest on money borrowed, except on money borrowed by way of bank overdraft or on mortgage from a Building Society or Local Authority, shall not exceed 6½% per annum, or 3% above the Bank of England Minimum Lending Rate, whichever is the higher.

(c) The Co-operative may receive from any persons donations or loans free of interest towards the work of the Co-operative.

(d) The Co-operative may receive any sums of money within the total limit mentioned in section (a) of this Rule, from Members and others on deposit, repayable on such notice being not less than 14 clear days, as they arrange from time to time, provided that such deposits shall be received in instalments of not more than £2 in any one payment or more than £50 in all from any one depositor.

10. MANAGEMENT

(a) There shall be regular General Meetings of all Members of the Co-operative. These shall be called by the Secretary giving each Member seven clear days notice of the date, time and place of the meeting and the issues upon which decisions are to be taken. The Secretary shall also call a meeting at the request of three or more Members delivered to him or her in writing.

(b) Each General Meeting shall elect a Chairman whose function will be to conduct the business of the meeting in an orderly manner.

(c) The Co-operative shall have a Committee of not less than five and not more than nineteen Committee Members, the number to be decided by a General Meeting. The Committee Members shall be elected each year at the Annual General Meeting. Retiring Committee Members shall be eligible for re-election without nomination. Nominations for the Committee shall be in writing and signed by two Members making the nomination and shall contain a statement by the Member nominated of his or her willingness to be elected. The nominations shall be delivered to the Secretary not less than seven days before the Annual General Meeting. Only Members shall be eligible to be Committee Members. Any Committee

Member may be removed from office by a majority vote at a General Meeting called for this purpose. Any remuneration of Committee Members shall be decided by Members in General Meeting. The Committee may exercise all such powers as may be exercised by the Co-operative and are not by these Rules or statute required to be exercised by the Co-operative in General Meeting, subject nevertheless to the provisions of these Rules and any regulations not inconsistent with these Rules made from time to time by the Co-operative in General Meeting.

(d) A General Meeting shall elect and may remove a Treasurer under their direction to be responsible for the proper management of the financial affairs of the Co-operative.

(e) A General Meeting shall elect and may remove a Secretary under their direction who will have those functions numerated in these Rules and such further functions as a meeting may determine.

(f) No business shall be contracted at any General Meeting unless one half or more of the Members are present.

11. VOTING. Every Member present in person at a General Meeting shall have one vote, and questions will be decided upon a majority vote of Members present except for those questions to be decided in accordance with Rule 17.

12. An ANNUAL GENERAL MEETING shall be held within six months of the close of the financial year of the Co-operative, the business of which will include:

(a) The receipt of the account and balance sheet.

(b) The appointment of an auditor.

(c) The election of Committee Members.

13. INVESTMENT OF FUNDS
The funds of the Co-operative may with the authority of the General Meeting be invested as follows:

(a) In or upon security in which trustees are for the time being authorised by law to invest; and

(b) In or upon any mortgage, bond, debenture, debenture stock, corporation stock, rent charge, rent or other security (not being securities payable to bearer) authorised by or under any Act of Parliament passed or to be passed of any Local Authority as defined by Section 34 of the Local Loans Act, 1875; and

(c) In the shares or on the security of any other society registered or deemed to be registered under the Act, or under the Building Societies Acts, or of any company registered under the Companies Acts, or incorporated by Act of Parliament or by Charter, provided that no such investment be made in the shares of any society or company other than one with limited liability.

The Co-operative may appoint any one or more of its Members to vote on its behalf at the meetings of any other body corporate in which the Co-operative has invested any part of its funds.

14. APPLICATION OF PROFITS: The profits of the Co-operative shall be applied as follows, in such proportions and in such manner as the General Meeting shall decide from time to time:

(a) Firstly, to a general reserve for the continuation and development of the Co-operative.
(b) Secondly, to a bonus to Members.
(c) Thirdly, to make payments for the social and charitable objects in connection with Rule 2.

15. AUDITORS

(a) The Co-operative shall in accordance with Sections 4 and 8 of the Friendly and Industrial and Provident Societies Act 1968 appoint in each year one or more auditors to whom the accounts of the Co-operative for that year shall be submitted for audit as required by the said Act, and who shall have such rights in relation to notice of an attendance and audience at General Meetings, access to books and the supply of information, and otherwise, as are provided by the said Act.

Every such auditor shall be appointed by the Co-operative in a General Meeting, and in the case of any auditor so appointed who is a qualified auditor under Section 7 of the said Act the provisions of Sections 5 and 6 thereof apply to his re-appointment and removal and to any resolution removing him or appointing another person in his place.

(b) Every year not later than the date provided by the Act or where the return is made up to the date allowed by the Registrar, not later than three months after such date, the Secretary shall send to the Registrar, the annual return in the form prescribed by the Chief Registrar of Friendly Societies relating to its affairs for the period required by the Act to be included in the return together with—

(1) a copy of the report of the auditor on the Co-operatives accounts for the period included in the return and

(2) a copy of each balance sheet made during that period and of the report of the auditor on that balance sheet.

16. RECORDS AND SEAL

(a) The Co-operative shall keep at its registered office a register of Members in which the Secretary shall enter the following particulars—

(1) the name and addresses of the Members;

(2) a statement of the number of shares held by each Member and of the amount paid or agreed to be considered as paid on the shares of each member;

(3) a statement of other property in the Co-operative, whether in loans, deposits or otherwise, held by each Member;

(4) the date at which each person was entered in the register as a Member, and the date at which any person ceased to be a Member;

(5) the names and addresses of the officers of the Co-operative, with the offices held by them respectively and the dates on which they assumed office.

Any Member changing his address shall notify the Co-operative.

(b) The Co-operative shall have a seal kept in the custody of the Secretary and used only by the authority of a General Meeting. Sealing shall be attested by the signatures of two Members and that of the Secretary for the time being.

17. AMENDMENTS TO RULES

(a) Any rule herein may be rescinded or amended or a new rule made by the vote of three quarters of all the Members of the co-operative at a General Meeting where all the Members of the Co-operative have been given seven clear days prior notice of the change to be proposed at that meeting.

(b) No amendment of rules is valid until registered.

18. DISSOLUTION: The Co-operative may be dissolved by the consent of threequarters of the Members by their signatures to an instrument of dissolution provided for in theTreasury Regulations or by winding up in a manner provided by the Act. If on the winding up or dissolution of the Co-operative any of its assets remain to be disposed of after its liabilities are satisfied, the assets shall not be distributed among the Members but shall be transferred to such a common ownership enterprise or such a central fund maintained for the benefit of common ownership enterprises, as may be determined by the Members at or before the time of the winding up or dissolution or, in so far as the assets are not so transferred, shall be held for charitable purposes.

19. DECEASED MEMBERS

(a) Upon a claim being made by the personal representative of a deceased Member or the trustee in bankruptcy of a bankrupt Member to any property in the Co-operative belonging to the deceased or bankrupt Member the Co-operative shall transfer or pay such property to which the personal representative or trustee in bankruptcy has become entitled as the personal representative or trustee in bankruptcy may direct them.

(b) A Member may in accordance with the Act nominate any person or persons to whom any of his property in the Co-operative at the time of his death shall be transferred but such nomination shall only be valid to the extent of the amount for the time being provided in the Act. On receiving satisfactory proof of death of a Member who has made a nomination the General Meeting shall, in accordance with the Act, either transfer or pay the full value of the property comprised in the nomination to the person entitled thereunder.

20. DISPUTES. Any such dispute as is referred to in Section 60(1) of the Industrial and Provident Societies Act 1965 shall be referred to and decided by the Chief Registrar of Friendly Societies.

21. In these rules 'The Act' refers to the Industrial and Provident Societies Acts 1965 to 1975 or any Act or Acts amending or in substitution for them for the time being in force.

Signatures of FOUNDER MEMBERS	Names in block letters
1.	....
2.	....
3.	....
4.	....
6.	....
7.	....
Secretary........................	....

REGISTRATION CERTIFICATE (to be affixed below)

Industrial and Provident Societies Act 1965 Registration of Societies

Societies which may be registered

1. A society qualifies for registration under the Act if:
   a. it is a society for carrying on an industry, business or trade and
   b. it satisfies the Registrar that either
      1) it is a bona fide co-operative society or
      2) in view of the fact that its business is being or is intended to be conducted for the benefit of the community there are special reasons why it should be registered under the Act rather than as a company under the Companies Act.

Bona fide co-operative societies

2. There is no statutory definition of a bona fide co-operative society but such a society will normally be expected to satisfy the following conditions:

   a. Conduct of business. The business of the society will be conducted for the mutual benefit of its members in such a way that the benefit which members obtain will in the main stem from their participation in its business. Such participation may vary in accordance with the nature of the society. It may consist of purchasing from or selling to the society, of using the services or amenities provided by it or of supplying services to carry out its business.

   b. Control. Control of the society will under its rules be vested in the members equally and not in accordance with their financial interest in the society. In general therefore the principle of 'one man, one vote' must obtain.

   c. Interest on share and loan capital. Interest payable on share and loan capital will under its rules not exceed a rate necessary to obtain and retain the capital required to carry out the objects of the society. The appropriate rate may vary from time to time between societies of different classes and according to the term and security of loans.

Section 1(3) of the Act provides that a society which carries on business with the object of making profits mainly for the payment of interest, dividends or bonuses on money invested with or lent to the society or any other person is not a bona fide co-operative society.

d. Profits. The profits of the society's business after payment of interest on share capital, if distributable amongst the members, will under its rules be distributable amongst them in relation to the extent to which they have traded with or taken part in the business of the society. Thus in a retail trading society or an agricultural marketing society profits will be distributable amongst members as a dividend or bonus on purchases from or sales to the society. In some societies (as for example social clubs) profits will not usually be distributable amongst members but are ploughed back to cheapen and improve the amenities available to members.

e. Restriction on membership. There should be no artificial restriction of membership with the object of increasing the value of proprietary rights and interests. There may, of course, be grounds for restricting membership that do not offend the co-operative principle; for example, the membership of a club might be limited by the size of its premises and of a self-build housing society by the number of houses that could be erected on a particular site.

Societies for the benefit of the community

3. To qualify for registration otherwise than as a bona fide co-operative society a society must satisfy two principal conditions:

   a. that its business will be conducted for the benefit of the community and

   b. that there are special reasons why it should be registered under the Act rather than as a company under the Companies Act.

4. A society claiming that it will be conducted for the benefit of the community must be able to show amongst other things that it will benefit persons other than its own members and that its business will be in the interests of the community. Typical societies which qualify for registration in this category are those which provide housing for various groups within the community, some (although not all) being charitable or philanthropic in character. In considering whether a society in this category should be registered regard will also be had to whether it is non-profit making and is prohibited by its rules from distributing its assets among members and to the matters referred to at b., c., and e. in paragraph 2 above.

Other conditions of registration

5. Every society seeking registration under the Act must also satisfy the following conditions:

a. unless the society consists of two or more registered societies it must have at least seven members;

b. the rules of the society must provide for all the matters required by Schedule 1 of the Act (these matters are set out in detail in the form of application for registration, form A, which may be obtained on application to the Registrar); and

c. the proposed name of the society must, in the opinion of the Registrar, not be undesirable. (The Registrar is prepared to indicate in advance of a formal application for registration whether a proposed name is, at that time, available).

6. The Registrar's certificate only certifies that a society is registered. It implies that the rules are in accordance with the Act but not that they are prudent, clear or well drafted. The responsibility in these matters rests on the society and its advisers. Great care should therefore be taken to have the rules settled in proper form.

Procedure for registration

7. Applications for registration must be in accordance with the requirements of the Act and of the Regulations made

thereunder. These requirements are referred to in form A (see paragraph 5b. above).

8. Model rules prepared by certain 'promoting bodies' will be accepted by the Registrar for registration. Applications using these model rules must be submitted through and endorsed by the secretary of the body concerned. A list of promoting bodies (F.280) is obtainable from the Registrar on demand.

9. If model rules of a promoting body are not to be adopted the proposed rules should be submitted to the Registrar in draft form for preliminary examination. Where the proposed rules are a copy of or are based upon rules of another society registered under the Act this should be stated.

10. The rules finally submitted for registration should be proof prints in book form, duly signed. The size is immaterial provided that it is not larger than A4 (210mm. × 297mm.) but there should be an adequate inner margin for purposes of filing.

11. The fee payable for an acknowledgement of registry of a society under the Act will depend upon whether application is made under paragraph 8 above or not. A note of the current fee (F. 823) is obtainable from the Registrar on demand.

Registry of Friendly Societies,
17, North Audley Street,
London, WIY 2AP

Notes on the Industrial Common Ownership (ICO) Act, with copy of the Act

The ICO Act is of interest to those contemplating the formation of workers' co-operatives principally because it enables government to provide money for two purposes; to finance advisory agencies (Sec. 1 (1)), and to enable loans to be made to co-operatives (Sec. 1 (2)).

To date (October 1979) funds under Sec. 1(1)) have been allocated to the Industrial Common Ownership Movement (ICOM) and the Scottish Co-operatives Development Committee (SCDC), and the money provided by Sec. 1 (2) is administered by Industrial Common Ownership Finance Ltd. (ICOF).

Those who drafted the act wished to define who may benefit from it, and to this end the act defines two types of enterprise, namely a Common Ownership Enterprise (Sec. 2 (1)), and a Co-operative Enterprise (Sec. 2 (2)).

Although the two organisations currently receiving funds under Sec. 1 (1) are willing to assist any enterprise which shows promise of adopting co-operative principles and practice, they both consider it desirable that such enterprises should be working towards compliance with one or other of the two definitions laid down by the act. Furthermore, ICOF is not permitted to make loans from money provided by Sec. 1 (2) except to enterprises which do comply with one of the two definitions and which hold a certificate to that effect, (though it does have other sources of finance from which it can make loans to bona fide co-operatives for which a certificate under the act is not a condition).

Evidently, therefore, there are advantages to be gained from the acquisition of a certificate under the act, either from the Registrar of Friendly Societies (RFS) as a Common Ownership Enterprise or from the Secretary of State for Industry as a Co-operative Enterprise. Which course is selected for any particular enterprise is a matter of choice by the members, and we set out below some of the factors which may affect that choice and notes on the application procedures.

The criteria by which the RFS will decide eligibility as a Common Ownership Enterprise are clearly defined in Sec. 2 (1). They follow closely the principles embodied in the ICOM Model Rules (1977) and it has in fact been established that the adoption of those rules will ensure recognition by the RFS under Sec. 2 (1), though their adoption is not obligatory for recognition.

If an enterprise decides to apply for a certificate as a Common Ownership Enterprise, Forms ICO 1 (Notes on the Act) and ICO 2 (Application Form) should be obtained from the RFS. Form ICO 2 is then completed and returned to the RFS together with a copy of the enterprise's rules, (if a company, copies of its Memorandum and Articles of Association and its latest balance sheet and accounts and those of any subsidiaries), and the Registrar's fee of £50 (reduced to £25 if ICOM Model Rules (1977) are adopted).

Sec. 2 (2) is less specific than Sec. 2 (1) and the Secretary of State has therefore produced 'Notes for Guidance' to assist those who choose to apply for recognition as a Co-operative Enterprise under Sec. 2 (2) rather than as a Common Ownership Enterprise under Sec. 2 (1). These notes are given below in full. The application procedure under Sec. 2 (2) is the same as for Sec. 2 (1) except that it is made to the Secretary of State instead of the RFS and the Secretary of State charges no fee. The ICOM Model Rules (1977) are acceptable for certification under Sec. 2 (2). Application forms can be obtained from the Secretary of State.

In both cases (RFS and Secretary of State) an annual return will have to be filed to ensure that certification continues to apply.

Department of Industry notes for the guidance of a body wishing to apply to the Secretary of State for a certificate that he is satisfied that it has the requisite characteristics of a co-operative enterprise.

1. Conditions for obtaining a certificate:
Attention is drawn to Section 2 (2) of the Act, which sets out the matter as to which the Secretary of State is required to be satisfied before issuing a certificate. Broadly, the applicant body must be in substance a co-operative association and it must be controlled by a majority of the people working for it (and for any subsidiaries).

2 (a). The essential characteristics of a co-operative association for this purpose are:
i) Membership
   a. Membership must, subject to any provision about membership by reference to age, length of service or other factors of any description which do not discriminate between persons by reference to politics or religion be open to all persons who work for the co-operative or for any of its subsidiaries.
   b. Membership may also be open to persons who use the products or services of the co-operative, to ex-employees of it or its subsidiaries, to relatives of any such existing or ex-employees and to other co-operative associations, but to no other persons.
ii) Control
   a. Control must be by the membership on the basis of one man, one vote, and in particular
   b. the investment of capital, either by way of shares or loans, must not deprive the membership of its ultimate control.
iii) Objects
   The co-operative must be operated primarily for the benefit of its members, and not, for example, primarily for the benefit of charity.
iv) Investment and Dividend
   a. Interest payable on share capital and loans must not be calculated by reference to profit rates.

b. The dividend paid to members must be a distribution of profit made in proportion to the work done for the co-operative or to the use made of its products or services, and must not be related to investment in the co-operative.

2 (b). An incorporated body fulfilling these criteria may be recognised as a co-operative enterprise only if it has 20 members or less. Any such body which carried on a business for gain and had more than 20 members would be an illegal association by virtue of Section 434 of the Companies Act 1948.

3. Bodies governed by the Industrial Common Ownership Movement Rules (ICOM 1977) will be regarded as satisfying these criteria if their members form a majority of the workforce.

4. Application for a certificate.
Where a body wishes to apply for a certificate, it should forward to the Department of Industry:
    a. A completed application form.
    b. When the applicant body is a company, a copy of the current Memorandum and Articles, and a copy of the latest accounts and balance sheet of the company, together with a copy of the current Memorandum and Articles and a copy of the latest account and balance sheet of any subsidiaries.
    c. When the applicant body is a Society, registered or deemed to be registered under the Industrial and Provident Societies Acts 1965-1975 a copy of the current Rules.

5. If it is found that the applicant body does not satisfy the requirements of Section 2 (2), the reasons for this will be indicated. In some cases further enquiry by the Department of Industry may be necessary before the matter can be fully determined. In other cases it may prove necessary for the body to make certain changes (e.g. amendment of the Rules or, as appropriate, of the Memorandum and Articles) before the certificate is given.

6. Revocation of certificates
There is no requirement that a certificate, once given, has to be renewed from time to time. However, under Section 2 (4) of the Act the Secretary of State may revoke a certificate if

it appears to him that a body in respect of which it has been given has ceased to be a co-operative enterprise. The Secretary of State will wish to be satisfied from time to time that a certificated body continues to qualify.

Department of Industry,
January 1978

ELIZABETH II

Industrial Common Ownership Act 1976

1976 CHAPTER 78

An Act to further the development of enterprises controlled by people working in them, and for purposes
connected therewith.   [22nd November 1976]

BE IT ENACTED by the Queen's most Excellent Majesty, by and
with the advice and consent of the Lords Spiritual and
Temporal, and Commons, in this present Parliament
assembled, and by the authority of the same, as follows:—

1.—(1) The Secretary of State may with the consent of the Grants and
Treasury, in the year beginning with the date when this Act loans.
comes into force and in each of the four following years, make
grants to any relevant body out of money provided by Parliament,
on such terms as he thinks fit, for the purpose of assisting the
body to provide advice about the organisation of common
ownership enterprises and co-operative enterprises; but the
aggregate amount of the grants made in pursuance of this subsection in any year shall not exceed £30,000.

(2) The Secretary of State may with the consent of the Treasury
make grants and loans to any relevant body out of money provided by Parliament, on such terms as he thinks fit, for the
purpose of assisting the body to make loans to common ownership enterprises and co-operative enterprises; but—

  (*a*) the aggregate amount of the grants made and the loans
      by the Secretary of State which are for the time being
      outstanding in pursuance of this subsection shall not
      exceed £250,000; and

(*b*) no grant or loan shall be made by the Secretary of State in pursuance of this subsection after the expiration of the period of five years beginning with the date when this Act comes into force.

(3) The Secretary of State may, by regulations made by statutory instrument, make provision with respect to the circumstances in which, the purposes for which and the terms on which money granted or lent by him to a body in pursuance of the preceding subsection may be lent by that body; and any statutory instrument made by virtue of this subsection shall be subject to annulment in pursuance of a resolution of either House of Parliament.

(4) Any sum received by the Secretary of State in repayment of a loan made by him in pursuance of subsection (2) of this section or by way of interest on such a loan shall be paid into the Consolidated Fund.

(5) In this section " relevant body " means a body appearing to the Secretary of State to be constituted for the purpose of encouraging the development of common ownership enterprises or co-operative enterprises.

Common ownership enterprises and co-operative enterprises.

2.—(1) For the purposes of this Act a common ownership enterprise is a body as to which the registrar has given, and has not revoked, a certificate stating that he is satisfied—

(*a*) that the body is—

(i) a company which has no share capital, is limited by guarantee and is a bona fide co-operative society; or

(ii) a society registered or deemed to be registered under the Industrial and Provident Societies Acts 1965 to 1975; and

(*b*) that the memorandum or articles of association or rules of the body include provisions which secure—

(i) that only persons who are employed by, or by a subsidiary of, the body may be members of it, that (subject to any provision about qualifications for membership which is from time to time made by the members of the body by reference to age, length of service or other factors of any description which do not discriminate between persons by reference to politics or religion) all such persons may be members of the body and that members have equal voting rights at meetings of the body,

(ii) that the assets of the body are applied only for the purposes of objects of the body which do not include the making over of assets to any member of the body except for value and except in pursuance of arrangements for sharing the profits of the body among its members, and

(iii) that, if on the winding up or dissolution of the body any of its assets remain to be disposed of after its liabilities are satisfied, the assets are not distributed among its members but are transferred to such a common ownership enterprise or such a central fund maintained for the benefit of common ownership enterprises as may be determined by the members at or before the time of the winding up or dissolution or, in so far as the assets are not so transferred, are held for charitable purposes; and

(c) that the body is controlled by a majority of the people working for the body and of the people working for the subsidiaries, if any, of the body.

(2) For the purposes of this Act a co-operative enterprise is a body as to which the Secretary of State has given, and has not revoked, a certificate stating that he is satisfied that—

(a) having regard to the provision which is made by the written constitution of the body as to the manner in which the income of the body is to be applied for the benefit of its members and all other relevant provisions of the constitution, the body is in substance a co-operative association; and

(b) the body is controlled by a majority of the people working for the body and of the people working for the subsidiaries, if any, of the body.

(3) The registrar may charge such a fee as the Treasury may determine for any certificate which he proposes to give in pursuance of this section, and any sum received by him in respect of such a fee shall be paid into the Consolidated Fund.

(4) If it appears to the registrar or the Secretary of State that a body in respect of which he has given a certificate in pursuance of this section has ceased to be a common ownership enterprise or a co-operative enterprise, he may revoke the certificate.

(5) In this section—

" company " means a company as defined by section 455(1) of the Companies Act 1948 or a company registered under that Act; and   1948 c. 38.

" the registrar " means the Chief Registrar within the meaning of the Friendly Societies Act 1974;   1974 c. 46.

and for the purposes of this section a body is a subsidiary of another body if it is a subsidiary of the other body for the purposes of the Companies Act 1948 or the Friendly and Industrial and 1968 c. 55. Provident Societies Act 1968.

Short title and extent.

3.—(1) This Act may be cited as the Industrial Common Ownership Act 1976.

(2) This Act shall not extend to Northern Ireland.

PRINTED IN ENGLAND BY HAROLD GLOVER
Controller of Her Majesty's Stationery Office and Queen's Printer of Acts of Parliament

Examples of budgets, with notes

GENERAL NOTES

Seven people (the founders) plan to set up a manufacturing business and to operate as a workers' co-operative. One of them is willing to give his services (free) as an organiser/ secretary for the first year, but the other six need to draw a wage. Since there are seven of them, they can if they wish register as a co-operative under the I & PS Acts. After much discussion and careful study of the market, costs, etc., they make the following assumptions:

Wages
For the first two years the six will each draw a wage of £50 p.w. (6 × 52 × £50 = £15,600), and will allow for an 'on cost' of 20% to cover payment of Employers' N.I. contributions, Employers' Liability Insurance, holidays with pay, sickness pay, etc. (20% × £15,600 = £3,120).

General overheads
They will rent premises, and allow £6,080 in the first year to cover all overheads such as rent, rates, insurances, telephone, electricity, plant maintenance, secretarial assistance, advertising, sales promotion, etc., etc. This is increased to £10,080 for the second year to allow for the fact that increased production will require an increase in general overheads, particularly since the seventh founder, though probably remaining a member and adviser, will be playing a less active role.

Materials
They expect to use £44,000 worth of materials in the first year and £60,000 in the second, and plan always to have £10,000 worth of materials in stock.

Plant
They plan to buy £10,000 worth of plant at the beginning of the first year and to write this off over five years. In simple terms it will all be worn out and need replacing after five

years, but in practice some of the money set aside for depreciation will be used for the renewal of plant within that five year period. (£10,000 ÷ 5 = £2,000). They might of course consider the hire purchase or lease of plant instead of outright purchase but whether they saved expenditure thereby would depend on what terms they were able to negotiate.

Interest
They expect to be able to borrow money for an indefinite period at approximately 13% p.a., interest to be paid twice yearly.

Income
They expect to produce readily saleable goods worth £80,000 in the first year and £108,000 in the second. (These figures are each approximately 1.8 × cost of materials).

Tax
They assume tax will be payable at 40%.

Using these figures, they try to make an estimate (budget) of the profit they might make in the first year, (see accompanying profit budget), but find they cannot complete it because they cannot fill in a figure for interest without knowing how much money they may need to borrow. They therefore make the following further approximate assumptions:

that in the first year money will be spent at an even rate on wages, 'on cost' and general overheads, i.e. at a rate of £24,800 ÷ 4 = £6,200 per quarter,

that materials will be used steadily at £44,000 ÷ 4 = £11,000 per quarter, that they will allow for depreciation at the end of each year, and that they will only get paid for £7,000 worth of goods in the first quarter.

They are now able to calculate that their outgoings in the first quarter might be £6,200 + £11,000 + £10,000 (for stock) + £10,000 (for plant) = £37,200, and since they hope to receive £7,000 they are likely to need to borrow about £31,000. To allow for unforeseen contingencies, they decide that they had better borrow £34,000, and at 13% this means that they will have to pay £4,400 p.a. in interst. They are now able to draw up profit and cash flow budgets for their first two years trading, which is as far as they feel able to look at present.

They decide:

From the profit budget
that over the first two years they might produce a surplus of about £10,000. This they can use for such purposes as reducing their loan, acquiring more assets to expand the business, distribution as bonus and donations. They will probably be wise to use it mostly for the first two purposes in the early years.

From the cash flow budget
that their need for finance should not exceed the £34,000 they plan to borrow, at any time during the first two years, and should in fact decrease slightly.

The decreasing loan requirement over the two years indicates that funds are available to repay part of the original loan of £34,000. The funds have, of course, been generated by the profitability of the enterprise as shown by the profit budget.

IMPORTANT

1. The figures used in these budgets are for illustrative purposes only. It should not be assumed that they represent a typical enterprise, and those planning an enterprise must use figures based on their own research, experience and judgement.

2. Simplified accounting methods have been used, and no account has been taken of any grants, special loans or tax concessions which may be available.

3. No account has been taken of inflation.

4. We wish to thank Mr. D. Taylor of the Business Studies Department, Carlisle Technical College, for his help in compiling this appendix.

Profit Budget

YEAR 1

EXPENDITURE			INCOME		
Wages	£	15,600	Sales	£	80,000
Wages 'on cost'		3,120			
Gen. Overheads		6,080			
		———			
Sub Total	£	24,800			
Materials Used		44,000			
Depreciation		2,000			
Interest		4,400			
		———	Less total		
Total	£	75,200	expenditure	£	75,200
					———
			Surplus before tax	£	4,800
			Less Tax @ 40%	£	1,900
					———
			TRADING SURPLUS	£	2,700

YEAR 2

EXPENDITURE			INCOME		
Wages	£	15,600	Sales	£	108,000
Wages 'on cost'		3,120			
Gen. Overheads		10,080			
		———			
Sub Total	£	28,800			
Materials Used		60,000			
Depreciation		2,000			
Interest		4,400			
		———	Less total		
Total	£	95,200	expenditure	£	95,200
					———
			Surplus before tax	£	12,800
			Less Tax @ 40%	£	5,100
					———
			TRADING SURPLUS	£	7,700

Cash Flow Budget

	YEAR 1				YEAR 2			
	1st Qr.	2nd Qr.	3rd Qr.	4th Qr.	5th Qr.	6th Qr.	7th Qr.	8th Qr.
Wages, on cost and Gen. O/H's	6,200	6,200	6,200	6,200	7,200	7,200	7,200	7,200
Materials	21,000	11,000	11,000	11,000	15,000	15,000	15,000	15,000
Plant (purchase)	10,000	-	-	-	-	-	-	-
Plant (depreciation)	-	-	-	2,000	-	-	-	2,000
Interest	-	2,200	-	2,200	-	2,200	-	2,200
Tax	-	-	-	1,900	-	-	-	5,100
Cash out	37,200	19,400	17,200	23,300	22,200	24,400	22,200	31,500
Cash in	7,000	20,000	20,000	20,000	22,000	27,000	27,000	27,000
Cash in — Cash out	(30,200)	600	2,800	(3,300)	(200)	2,600	4,800	(4,500)
Loan Requirement	30,200	29,600	26,800	30,100	30,300	27,700	22,900	27,400

Notes on Cash Flow Budget

1. Although £44,000 of materials are used during the first year, the quarterly totals add up to £54,000 because of the intention to carry £10,000 worth in stock.

2. For simplicity, tax for each year is shown as being paid in the last quarter of the year in which it was incurred. In practice, it would not be paid until some time later.

3. Under 'cash in' the inevitable delay between production and payment has been allowed for. Although £80,000 worth of goods are made in the first year, only £67,000 income is shown as received, and a similar allowance, which takes into account the increased production, has been made in the second year.

4. Bracketed figures represent negatives, i.e. more cash going out than coming in.

5. Loan requirement is a cumulative (algebraic) addition of the figures in the previous line, taking account of the brackets.

6. It will be prudent to pay the £4,000 shown for depreciation into an account (deposit, Buiding Society, etc.), separate from the main trading bank account. It will then earn some interest, (not included in this budget), and will be available when needed for plant renewal.

APPENDIX F
INDUSTRIAL COMMON OWNERSHIP FINANCE LTD.

Information for Loan Applicants, Prospectus Requirements, copy of Loan Application Form and Department of Industry guidelines for assessing projects

What money is available?
I.C.O.F. lending funds come from the Government - £250,000 available between 1977 and 1981 - and from sympathetic individuals and from successful co-operatives. £180,392 was on loan at December 1979 and more is becoming available year by year.

I.C.O.F. loans are typically for amounts between £2,500 and £10,000 although applications for sums up to £50,000 will be considered. Loans of less than £500 cannot be handled.

I.C.O.F. loans are short to medium term - from six months to six years - and repayments can be at regular periods throughout the life of the loan or in one lump sum at the end.

Sometimes an enterprise might negotiate a private loan which can be channeled through I.C.O.F. who will see to necessary documentation. Before accepting such an ear-marked loan for processing I.C.O.F. will apply its usual criteria of viability.

Who may apply?
Loans can only be made to incorporated bodies and only to those with a common-ownership or co-operative structure. Typically this will take the form of a registered co-operative society (probably using the I.C.O.M. model rules) or of a company limited by guarantee without shares and with appropriate articles of association. An enterprise with any other legal structure will need to satisfy the I.C.O.F. Trustees that it is genuinely a co-operative.

Applicants to the general I.C.O.F. fund should be members of the Industrial Common Ownership Movement (I.C.O.M.) and satisfy I.C.O.F. that they are in practice as well as in structure a co-operative.

Applicants to the Government fund must:

★ at least in part of their operation be manufacturing a product rather than only providing a service.

★ obtain a certificate stating that they are a bona-fida co-operative - that is, under the terms of the Industrial Common Ownership Act 1976 that more than half of the people working in an enterprise are full voting members of it. Certificates should be obtained either from the Registrar of Friendly Societies or from the Secretary of State for Industry. The Registrar has accepted that the I.C.O.M. model rules meet the requirements of the Act and charges a model rules co-op a substantially lower fee for its I.C.O. Act certificate.

★ obtain a letter of support from their relevant trades union.

How is application made?

★ make contact with the I.C.O.F. Secretary, who will discuss the proposed application and give necessary advice and guidance. In particular he will advise if the enterprise might qualify for a loan from the government fund.

★ complete an I.C.O.F. loan application form.

★ prepare a **prospectus** as detailed on the reverse of the I.C.O.F. application form.

★ attach audited accounts (where available).

★ for loans from the Government fund obtain an I.C.O. Act certificate and a Trades Union letter of support.

The I.C.O.F. Secretary will generally visit applicant enterprises before their case is considered by the Trustees in order to form a first hand impression and to ensure that the Trustees have all the information they require in order to make a decision.

In some situations I.C.O.F. will invite applicants to attend a Trustees meeting to present their case in person.

How much will it cost?

I.C.O.F. interest rates are reviewed twice a year in April and October. It is I.C.O.F. policy to maintain a steady rate of interest rather than change frequently in line with the minimum lending rate. The rate fixed in October 1979 was 12%

Interest is payable twice yearly in June and December.

How will I.C.O.F. judge the application?

As well as looking for evidence of co-operative structure and spirit, I.C.O.F. Trustees will want to satisfy themselves that an applicant enterprise is a viable concern with reasonable prospects of success. In particular attention will be paid to marketing organisation, organisational efficiency and the adequacy of financial control and information systems.

(For full details of criteria applied, see **Guidelines for assessing projects**, produced by the Department of Industry and attached.)

I.C.O.F. will sometimes seek evidence of financial commitment by members to their enterprise either through initial loans or through the regular ploughback of a percentage of wages.

Will I.C.O.F. impose any conditions?

★ I.C.O.F. will normally request regular financial information as a basis for monitoring the financial health of the borrowing co-operative.

★ In some cases I.C.O.F. will wish to ensure that the co-operative is adequately advised.

Must security be provided for the loan?

In most cases I.C.O.F. will seek some form of security for any loan: usually through a registered debenture. Exceptionally I.C.O.F. will make a loan where no security is available but where trading prospects appear to be very sound.

Time limit on loan offer?

Loan offers remain valid for a period of three months. After the expiry date a letter of withdrawal is sent and the case is re-presented for review, drawing attention to changes, if any, from the original application.

How long will it take?

The trustees meet every quarter, and an Advances Sub-committee meets each month. If all documentation is ready and there are no problems an application can be processed within a month. More usually the process will take between eight and twelve weeks.

Is there any appeal?

Decisions taken by the Sub-committee may be referred to the full Board of Trustees either by the Sub-committee or by the applicant. The Trustees decision is final and their normal practice is to give their reasons to unsuccessful applicants.

GUIDELINES FOR ASSESSING PROJECTS

Regulation 3(2) of the Industrial Common Ownership (Loans) regulations 1977 (Statutory Instrument 1977 No 1368) requires that an appraisal should be conducted by a relevant body before it makes a grant assisted loan. The amount of assistance given should be a minimum necessary to enable the project to go ahead. The relevant body must be satisfied that the project has a reasonable chance of success before making the loan.

The purpose of the appraisal is to make an assessment of viability, judging the amount of assistance required and the degree of risk. The following factors are among the relevant considerations:

1. Financial and commercial data.

   The relevant body should examine adequate and properly analysed data relating to the past records (if any) of the applicant enterprise (if possible over the previous 3 years trading), its current position and future trading estimates.

2. Market prospects.

   There should be a realistic appraisal of the market for the product(s) of the applicant enterprises, at home and overseas, and of the enterprise's ability to sell in these markets at competitive prices.

3. Managerial ability.

   The quality of management available is a crucial factor in assessing prospects of viability.

4. Product development.

   A successful product may lead to undue complacency if management is weak and fails to allow for a changing market.

5. In preparing forecasts the impact of inflation should be taken into account.

6. Other finance.

   If the applicant enterprise has other sources of finance and is putting up a substantial amount from its own resources or private outside finance, this may indicate a diminution of risk.

7. Industrial relations.

   Account should be taken of the policy and recent history of industrial relations in the applicant enterprise. The views of Trade Unions should be carefully considered. Without their co-operation there must be serious doubts about the viability of the enterprise and considerable weight must therefore be given to any indication that support might not be forthcoming.

8. Risk factors.

   The principal risks involved in the forecasts should be identified. The effect of these risk factors (such as changes in sales volume, prices, etc) on profit and cash flow should be calculated.

9. Security for loan.

   The present charges (if any) and security available should be verified.

Small Firms Division,
Department of Industry

I.C.O.F.

LOAN APPLICATION FORM
and
PROSPECTUS REQUIREMENTS

INDUSTRIAL COMMON OWNERSHIP
FINANCE LTD.

PROSPECTUS REQUIREMENTS

A **Prospectus** should be prepared to accompany the application form overleaf giving the following information:

A. FINANCIAL REPORT
1. Budget: profit and loss a/c
2. Month by month cash flow reflecting p&l a/c.
3. Statement of financing showing:

   * net assets in use
   * how financed – where the capital has come from
   * securities already pledged to other lenders

B. GENERAL REPORT
1. Introduction: background and history of the enterprise
2. The people: number, age-group, full/part-time, skills, background etc.
3. The common-ownership structure – how it works in practice
4. The product(s) and/or the service(s)
5. The market(s)
6. The management structure
7. Financial control and information systems
8. Future prospects and possible developments.

****

I.C.O.F. LOAN APPLICATION FORM

Important: this form should be completed **after** reading the ICOF leaflet **Information for loan applicants.**

1. name and address of enterprise:

   telephone number

2. **legal status:** Please state whether registered co-operative or company limited by guarantee, or other, and give registration/company number:

3. **certificate under ICO Act:** Has the enterprise received a certificate under the Industrial Common Ownership Act 1976? Please give date of application or receipt as appropriate and whether to/ from Registrar of Friendly Societies or Sec. of State for Industry:

4. **Trades Union support:** Has the enterprise received a letter of support from a relevant local Trades Union?

5. **number of workers:** How many people are working in the enterprise?
   full-time
   part-time

6. How many people do you expect to be working in the enterprise three years from now?

7. **membership:** How many workers are full voting members of the enterprise?

8. **ICOM:** Is the enterprise a member of the Industrial Common Ownership Movement? Please state if a Member Company or an Associate Member:

9. **product/service;** What is/are the main product(s)/service(s) of the enterprise?

10. **turnover:** What is the projected turnover for the current (or first) year of trading?

11. **banker's name:** Please state the name and address of the enterprise's bank:

12. **ICOF loan:** What size of loan is requested from ICOF?

13. Over what period and at what rate is it proposed to repay the loan?

14. For what specific purpose is the loan required? (e.g. working capital, premises, plant and machinery etc.)

15. What security might be offered?

signature

position in enterprise

date

Do not forget to send your BUSINESS PROSPECTUS   as well (see over).

APPENDIX G

Selected bibliography about co-operation and co-operatives

1. *A Century of Co-operation;* G.D.H. Cole; Co-operative Union; 1945
2. *British Co-operation;* A. Bonner; Co-operative Union; 1970
3. *Small is Beautiful;* E.F. Schumacher; Blond and Briggs; 1973
4. *Sharing our Industrial Future;* R. Sawtell; Industrial Society; 1968
5. *Self-management: Economic liberation of Man;* Ed. Jaroslav Vanek; Penguin; 1975
6. *The New Worker Co-operatives;* Ed. K. Coates; Institute for Workers'Control; 1976
7. *Towards a Worker Managed Economy;* Jeremy Bray and Nicholas Falk; Fabian Tract 430; April 1974
8. *Industrial Common Ownership;* David Watkins; Fabian Tract 455; April 1978
9. *Employment, Inflation and Politics;* Peter Jay; Institute for Economic Affairs Occasional Paper 46; 1976
10. *Workers' Participation in Co-operatives;* Society for Co-operative Studies; Bulletin 26; 1976
11. *An Industrial Co-operative Experiment in Cumbria;* J.Pearce; Papers in Community Studies No. 13; University of York; 1977
12. *The Story of the Scottish Daily News;* Ron McKay and Brian Barr; Canongate; 1976
13. Monographs published by the Co-operative Research Unit of the Open University:
    i. *Fakenham Enterprises;* Martin Lockett; 1978
    ii. *Fairblow Dynamics;* Rob Paton with Martin Lockett; 1979
    iii. *Some problems of Co-operative organisation;* Rob Paton; 1979
14. *Worker Owners - the Mondragon Achievement;* Campbell, Keene, Norman and Oakeshott; Anglo-German Foundation for the study of Industrial Society; 1978
15. Booklets published by the Industrial Common Ownership Movement:
    i. *Shop floor democracy in action; a personal account of the Coventry gang system;* Dwight Layton; 1972
    ii. *Trades unions and Common Ownership;* John Anagnostelis and Paul Derrick; 1972
    iii. *Workers' Self-Management in France;* Roger Hadley; 1973
    iv. *Worker Ownership;* Alastair Campbell; 1976

    v. *The Mondragon Movement;* Alastair Campbell and Blair Foster; 1974

   vi. *Sources of Finance for small Co-operatives;* John Pearce; 1979

  vii. *Industrial co-operatives - a guide to the ICOM Model Rules;* Roger Sawtell; 1977

 viii. *The Co-operative Way;* Antoine Antoni; 1980

16. *Community co-operatives - A guide;* Highlands and Islands Development Board; 1978

17. *Starting a co-operative;* John Lewis; Scottish Co-operatives Development Committee; 1979

18. *How to Convert a Company into an Industrial Co-operative;* R. Sawtell; Co-operative Development Agency; 1979

19. *Handbook to the Industrial and Provident Societies Act and Supplement;* W.J. Chappenden; Co-operative Union; 1966

20. *Co-operatives and Community;* D. Wright; Bedford Square Press; 1979

21. *In the Making;* a Directory of Co-operative Projects; No. 6; I.T.M. 1979

ABOUT THE AUTHORS

Peter Cockerton is an industrial accountant and has been involved with co-operatives and common-ownerships since 1971. He was a founder member of Arjuna Limited, one of the first co-operatives to use the ICOM Model Rules, and is currently a council member of ICOM. He has recently completed a feasability study into the formation of a local co-operative development agency in Milton Keynes.

Tim Gilmour-White worked for 25 years in the north of Scotland, initially as a civil engineer on the hydro-electric schemes and subsquently as a farmer in Ross-shire. His involvement in the Job Creation Project sponsored by the local District Council led him to a study of workers' co-operatives and to the writing for the Scottish Council of Social Service of the Scottish Handbook on which this handbook is based.

John Pearce first became involved with co-operatives when working on a Tibetan refugee resettlement project in Nepal. He is now Organiser of the Local Enterprise Advisory Project in the West of Scotland, is Secretary of the Scottish Co-operatives Development Committee and has been a Trustee of Industrial Common Ownership Finance Limited since 1976.

Anna Whyatt has worked in and with small-scale worker co-operatives since helping to establish Suma, a wholesale wholefood co-operative in Leeds, in 1975. She now works in employment development at local community level with a special brief to develop co-operative enterprises. She has lectured for several years on co-operative development for the Workers' Educational Association and as an occasional lecturer at the University of Bradford. She is joint secretary of the Yorkshire Co-operative Development Group.

NOTES

NOTES

NOTES